Hiram Bingham

and the Dream of Gold

Hiram Bingham

and the Dream of Gold

by Daniel Cohen

M. EVANS AND COMPANY, INC.
New York

Thanks are due to the publisher for permission to reprint selections from *Lost City of the Incas* by Hiram Bingham. Copyright 1948 by Duell, Sloan and Pearce. Renewal, 1976, by Alfred Bingham. Reprinted by permission of E. P. Dutton, Inc.

The author thanks Ernesto Busse, Director, Peru National Tourist Office, for permission to use the photograph of Machu Picchu as it appears today, and the Division of Anthropology, Yale Peabody Museum of Natural History, for permission to reprint the photographs from Hiram Bingham's expeditions.

Library of Congress Cataloging in Publication Data

Cohen, Daniel.
   Hiram Bingham and the dream of gold.

   Bibliography: p. 177
   Includes index.
   Summary: A biography of the man who discovered Machu Picchu in 1911 and later gave up his scholarly exploration to pursue a career in politics, taking a seat in the U.S. Senate after a two-day term as Governor of Connecticut.
   1. Bingham, Hiram, 1875–1956—Juvenile literature.
2. Incas—Juvenile literature. 3. Machu Picchu (Peru)—
Juvenile literature. 4. Explorers—America—Biography—
Juvenile literature. 5. Legislators—United States—
Biography—Juvenile literature. 6. United States.
Congress. Senate—Biography—Juvenile literature.
[1. Bingham, Hiram, 1875–1956. 2. Explorers.
3. Legislators. 4. Incas. 5. Indians of South America.
6. Machu Picchu (Peru)] I. Title.
F3429.B633C64   1984   985'.37 [92]   84-8177

ISBN 0-87131-433-9

M. Evans and Company, Inc.
216 East 49 Street
New York, New York 10017

Design by Lauren Dong

Manufactured in the United States of America
9 8 7 6 5 4 3 2 1

Contents

for Judy Kolbas

Acknowledgments

I would like to thank Judith Schiff and the staff of the Manuscripts and Archives Room at Yale's Sterling Library for all the help they gave me in consulting the Bingham family papers. I would also like to thank Dr. Leopold Pospisil, director of the Division of Anthropology at Yale, who gave me permission to examine the extensive photograph collection of the Yale Peruvian expedition. Special thanks are due to David Kiphuth of the Yale Peabody Museum of Natural History, who actually guided me into the vault where the collection is stored. I am grateful to the Peabody Museum for permission to reproduce the pictures from the expedition that appear in this book.

CHAPTER 1

"An Unbelievable Dream"

On the morning of July 24, 1911, Hiram Bingham was about to make the greatest discovery of his life—in fact, it would be the greatest archaeological discovery that has ever been made in the Americas. But as the day dawned in a cold drizzle, there were no signs or portents of what was to come in just a few hours.

The weather was so miserable that Melchor Arteaga, the farmer who had first told the members of the expedition about Inca ruins in the mountains, didn't even want to leave his hut. It was only after Bingham offered him a Peruvian golden *sol*, three times the usual guide's fee, that the farmer reluctantly agreed to go.

Other members of the Yale expedition had no faith in Arteaga's story, especially on so wet and chilly a morning. When the farmer had been asked where the ruins were, he just pointed straight up. They had heard similar rumors of ruins and had scrambled up and down mountains only to be disappointed. Harry Foote, the naturalist, decided that there were "more butterflies near the river" and that he was going to stay and collect them. Dr. William Erving, the surgeon, said he had to wash and mend his clothes. Besides, it was Bingham who had really dragged all of them into the Peruvian jungle to look for lost cities of gold, so finding the ruins was really his responsibility. He was the one who was supposed to follow through on every rumor, no matter how unpromising. And this rumor was an unpromising one indeed, for as far as they knew no one else had ever reported Inca ruins in this area of the Urubamba River.

So at about ten o'clock, Bingham, accompanied by Arteaga and the Peruvian officer Sergeant Carrasco, started off on the forested trail that followed the course of the Urubamba. Bingham saw a recently killed snake along the side of the road. It was yellowish in color and had a triangular pointed head. He asked Carrasco what sort of snake it was.

"Viper," replied the sergeant. Bingham knew that meant fer-de-lance, the lance-headed, or yellow, viper, the deadliest snake in the world and an aggressive killer that was known to actually spring through the air in pursuit of its victims. Carrasco casually mentioned that these "vipers" were quite common in the area. Bingham shuddered and walked more quickly.

The trail led through a spectacular landscape that Bingham would write about: "Great snow peaks loom[ed] above the clouds more than two miles overhead and gigantic precipices of many-colored granite [rose] sheer thousands of feet above the foaming, glistening, roaring rapids." On the peaks above, glaciers shimmered through the clouds. Below the peaks was dense tropical jungle. Along the road grew gigantic tree ferns, and orchids bloomed on their trunks and in their spreading branches. It was a land of unsurpassed beauty and great danger.

After about three-quarters of an hour of walking, Arteaga left the road and plunged through the jungle to the riverbank. He gestured somewhat uncertainly to a "bridge" that crossed the turbulent Urubamba at its narrowest point. The bridge was really a series of logs that spanned the gaps between boulders that stuck up out of the rapids. In his travels through the mountains of South America, Bingham had seen many primitive and rickety bridges. This was surely the worst. As he noted later, "The 'bridge' was made of half a dozen very slender logs, some of which were not long enough to span the distance between the boulders but had been spliced and fashioned together with vines!"

The river boiled up just a few feet beneath the bridge, and the logs were slippery and moss covered. Bingham knew that with one misstep he would plunge to an instant death in the icy rapids. Arteaga and the sergeant took off their shoes and crept carefully across, gripping the logs with their toes. Bingham, who was not used to gripping anything with his toes, adopted a different method. He got down on all fours and crawled across, a few inches at a time. Though he was a college teacher of history, this was no place to try to look dignified. As soon as he got across, instead of being relieved, he began to worry about how he was going to get back. The bridge was already under siege by the rapids. If it rained the frail logs would be washed away entirely.

Once again the trio plunged into the jungle, and in a few minutes they reached the base of a mountain, which seemed to Bingham, at least, to rise straight up. For the next hour and a half they climbed and clawed their way up several thousand feet. "For a good part of the distance we went on all fours, sometimes holding on by our fingernails."

The sergeant was grateful that his heavy boots were snakebite proof. But Arteaga worried and continued to talk loudly about snakes. After a while, Bingham began to wonder if a mere snakebite would not come as a welcome relief. Both the heat and the humidity were tremendous, and as Bingham discovered, he was in no shape for such a climb. He struggled for breath and swore that every foot of the climb would be his last. Worse still, there was no sign of ruins. There were signs that the area had once been inhabited or used as a trail. In one spot, the climbers found a notched tree trunk that served as a primitive ladder. But such signs were recent in origin. The whole venture might be a complete fiasco.

By noon Bingham was convinced that he was not going to be able to go any farther, that if the Lost City of the Incas itself lay at the top of the mountain, he would not have the strength or will to reach it. And then, amazingly, the climbers came upon a grass-covered hut inhabited by two very good-natured Indians who offered them gourds filled with cool, delicious water. To the exhausted Bingham the sight of the two smiling men holding out the overflowing gourds was like a vision, a dream. It was the first of a series of dreamlike experiences he was to have that day.

Over a lunch of boiled sweet potatoes, the two Indian farmers, Richarte and Alvarez, explained that they were able to grow a variety of crops—potatoes, beans, peppers, and tomatoes—on terraces that had been built into the mountainside. Why had they chosen to live in such a remote spot? The two men laughed and said that up here they were safe from the tax collectors and from army men looking for "volunteers." They went into the valley about once a month along the path that Bingham and his companions had just climbed or, during the rainy season when the bridge was washed out, along a path that was even steeper. Bingham found it difficult to imagine what that path might be like.

Bingham had stretched his six-foot-four frame out on a soft woolen poncho spread in the shade; he was enjoying the view. Thousands of feet below, looking like a twisting, shiny ribbon was the Urubamba River. On the other side of the valley was a sheer granite cliff, rising at least two thousand feet, and off to the left was the peak known as Huayna Picchu, surrounded by other, nameless peaks. All around were even higher, snow-capped mountains.

Bingham found this all so pleasant and so comfortable that he seriously considered not going any farther that day. But he finally roused himself and asked about the ruins.

Oh yes, ruins, the farmers replied rather absently, there were some just a little higher up. Since Richarte and Alvarez were farming on terraces that had been built by the Incas, it was reasonable to assume that other Inca structures would be found in the vicinity. But Bingham didn't really expect to find anything more interesting than a few broken-down stone houses. Arteaga decided not to visit the ruins because he had been there before. Richarte and Alvarez wanted to stay and gossip with Arteaga, for they didn't get much news in their eagle's nest home. But miraculously there appeared a small boy who offered to act as guide.

And so, led by the boy and followed by Sergeant Carrasco, Bingham started out once again. The sergeant was duty bound to follow Bingham, but he was now becoming quite curious as to what these "ruins" might be like.

Bingham had scarcely left the hut when he was confronted by an unexpected sight. Rising above him was a great flight of beautifully worked stone terraces, as many as one hundred of them, each hundreds of feet long and at least ten feet high. These terraces, built by the Incas centuries earlier, had been partially cleared of jungle by Richarte and Alvarez. The soil that the Incas had placed in the terraces was still capable of producing a rich crop.

Bingham was surprised by the number and size of the terraces, but he told himself it was nothing to get excited about. He had seen lots of terraces already but no lost cities. Still, he now felt less fatigued and followed his small guide eagerly. Beyond the portions of the terraces that had been cleared by Richarte and Alvarez, the jungle took over, and through the bamboo thickets and tangled vines, Bingham could see the walls of ancient houses built with superb Inca craftsmanship.

In Bingham's own words, "Suddenly without warning, under a huge overhanging ledge the boy showed me a cave beautifully lined with the finest cut stone. It had evidently been a royal mausoleum." That was only the start of the wonders. Half hidden in the vegetation was a building that closely resembled the famed Inca Temple of the Sun in Cuzco. Connected to it was a wall cut from the purest fine-grained white granite. "It seemed like an unbelievable dream. Dimly I began to realize that this wall and its adjoining semicircular temple over the cave were as fine as the finest stonework in the world."

By now Bingham was moving as if he were in a dream. The boy pointed to a flight of granite steps, and after a short walk along a path, Bingham found himself

standing in front of two beautiful white granite buildings, constructed from gigantic stones, some over six feet
high, which were fitted together with such care that the
blade of a knife could not be inserted between the blocks.

Bingham ran his hands over the exquisitely cut granite blocks, the largest of which must have weighed fifteen
tons. Would anyone believe what he had found? He
could scarcely believe it himself. "Fortunately, in this
land where accuracy of reporting what one has seen is
not a prevailing characteristic of travellers, I had a good
camera and the sun was shining."

There were more temples and plazas to be seen and
photographed, far too many to be photographed in a
single day. Bingham had not discovered a few ruined
buildings; he had discovered an entire city! A city that
was not on any map, that had never been mentioned in
any of the reports or chronicles written hundreds of
years ago by the Spanish conquerors of Peru.

The city was nestled in a saddle between two peaks,
Huayna Picchu to the north and the even higher Machu
Picchu to the south. Four thousand feet below flowed the
Urubamba. The city had no name, but it would come to
be known as Machu Picchu, after the taller of the two
peaks.

Bingham walked about taking pictures and wonder-
ing what he had really discovered. An Inca city certainly, but not a ruined city like all the other Inca cities in
Peru. This was an abandoned city. It was as if one day
the Incas had simply walked away from this place, leaving it to the jungle. And since that day it had remained
untouched and lost to the outside world. Aside from the
effects of time and vegetation the unknown city was intact. There was nothing else like it in South America,

nothing else like it in the entire world. What city could be so secret that its location never would have been mentioned in any of the chronicles?

Bingham's first thought was that he had finally found the fabled lost city of Vilcapampa, the secret capital of the great Inca resistance leader Manco and his sons, the last Incas. But that day Bingham also located a very singular structure, a temple with three great windows, quite unlike anything else built by the Incas in Peru. He remembered an old chronicle that stated that the first Inca, also called Manco, had a building with three windows constructed at the place of his birth. Could this hidden city he had discovered be both the birthplace and the tomb of the magnificent and mysterious Incas?

Hiram Bingham was determined to find out.

CHAPTER 2

The Lost Cities of the Incas

In 1532 a small Spanish expedition of tough, heavily armed men under the leadership of Francisco Pizarro came into contact with a magnificent and previously unknown empire in South America—the empire of the Incas. It was the last great empire totally unknown to the outside world.

The empire of the Incas had developed in isolation from the rest of the world and was an utterly unique society. Twelve years before Pizarro's expedition, another small group of Spanish, led by Hernando Cortes, had conquered the empire of the mighty Aztecs in Mexico. The Spanish had been steadily extending their control throughout Central and South America. The Incas knew nothing of this. The Spanish who had been making forays up and down the coasts of Central and South America for over twenty years had picked up vague rumors of the empire of the Incas. The rumors seemed fantastic; besides, there were always rumors filtering out from the interior, and there was no particular reason to believe this one.

Yet the empire was there. It covered hundreds of thousands of square miles from Quito in what is now Ecuador southward to the northern part of Argentina and central Chile. The Inca Empire spanned deserts, jungles, and mountains—mostly mountains. The center of the Inca Empire was in the high Andes in what is now Peru. It was the only empire in history ever to develop at such a high altitude. The Incas and many of their subjects were people specially adapted to life in the thin air of the Peruvian highlands. They were a stocky folk with barrel chests containing very large lungs that allowed them to breathe easily at altitudes which most flatlanders are unable to endure without a long period of acclimatization. Today a malnourished Peruvian Indian whose ancestors had served the Incas can carry a heavy load over the mountains, while the strongest visitor can barely put one foot in front of the other without gasping for breath.

To tie together their vast domain, the Incas had constructed a system of roads superior to anything that had been built in Europe since the time of the Romans. Even the Romans had never attempted to build roads over mountainous terrain such as the Andes. Yet the Incas had no wheeled vehicles, the wheel was completely unknown to them, and they had no beasts of burden except the llama, which cannot be ridden or carry very much.

The great secret of the Incas was their genius for organization. They could effectively set thousands of workers to building structures that rivaled in grandeur the pyramids of Egypt. When the Spanish first saw the Inca capital of Cuzco, they thought it finer than any city in Europe. By carefully terracing the land, the Incas could grow crops in places where any "sane" person would have said agriculture was impossible. Some of the vegetables now eaten every day—the potato, the tomato, and many others—came by way of the Incas.

By employing a relay of runners stationed at post houses along the great highway system, the Incas could send a message from one end of the empire to the other in just a few days. The emperor could sit in his palace at Cuzco and know the exact number of his subjects in the most distant village of the most distant province, and he could know to the day the amount of tribute labor each of the hundreds of villages in the empire owed every month. Yet the Incas had not even mastered the rudiments of writing as had the Aztecs and the Mayans, and as had some of the North American Indians of less highly developed cultures. All the elaborate Inca record keeping was done by means of the *quipu*—an arrangement of knotted colored yarn—which was used as a mnemonic, or memory-jogging, device.

For all of its organizational genius, the empire constructed by the Incas had a flaw, a fatal one, as it turned out. The empire was an autocracy. All the power was in the hands of a single individual—the emperor himself. The word *Inca* really means "king" or "emperor," and strictly speaking, there was only one Inca—the Inca, or the Lord Inca, who was both king and god for the people of the empire. He was regarded as a direct descendant of the sun. The Inca's word was divine law, it could not be questioned, appealed, or overruled. The Inca administered his laws through a bureaucracy of nobles chosen from among his many relatives. The nobles too came to be called Incas, but the only one who had any real power was *the Inca*. All the others served at his pleasure.

Though the Inca was regarded as divine by his subjects, and the carefully preserved mummies of dead Incas were venerated and treated as if they were still alive, the Inca was, of course, human. When the Inca died, there was a sudden and violent break in the continuity of the empire. The Incas had no clear line of succession, and theoretically any one of the dead Inca's sons could proclaim himself Lord Inca. The Incas had many wives and many children, so there were usually several brothers struggling for power, with the winner gaining the right to be Inca. It was an effective way of eliminating weaklings and fools from the line of succession, a sort of survival of the fittest struggle. The result was a series of remarkably able rulers. It also meant that the Inca Empire was regularly gripped by periods of great instability and uncertainty as brother eliminated brother.

Pizarro was extraordinarily lucky, for when he landed in Peru just such a succession crisis had occurred. The great Inca Huayna Capac had died suddenly, leaving two of his sons, Huáscar and Atahualpa, with excellent claims to supreme power. Huáscar was in control of the capital city of Cuzco, while Atahualpa was in command of the majority of the Inca army, which was stationed at Quito in the northern part of the empire.

For a while a sort of uneasy truce existed between the two brothers, but in a land where divided power was unknown the truce couldn't last, and inevitably civil war broke out. This war was an exceptionally vicious and bloody one, for while Huáscar had the loyalty of most of the empire, Atahualpa had the loyalty of the army, and in the end it was the might of the army that prevailed. Atahualpa's troops defeated those loyal to Huáscar outside Cuzco, and Huáscar himself was captured in the battle. Atahualpa with his enormous retinue was resting in the mountains near a city called Cajamarca, savoring his victory and planning his triumphal entry into Cuzco when news reached him of an unusual occurrence in his domain. A small group of bearded strangers who sat atop huge, fierce-looking beasts and who carried sticks that shot "thunder and lightning" were marching toward Cajamarca.

Atahualpa was not at all alarmed by this news, and he allowed the strangers to continue their progress unhampered, finally agreeing to meet them at Cajamarca. To Atahualpa the meeting was to be a momentary diversion, nothing more. Perhaps the strangers might even prove somehow useful. What had the Inca to fear? He had just prevailed in the most vicious war the world (at least the world as he knew it) had ever seen. He was surrounded by a well-trained army that numbered in the tens of thousands—while the strangers numbered a mere 150. As far as Atahualpa knew, at that moment he was the most powerful person in the universe.

Atahualpa decided to turn the meeting into a ceremonial procession in order to impress the strangers. He entered Cajamarca accompanied by six thousand gorgeously attired retainers. The bulk of the army remained outside the town, and the Inca's escort was mostly unarmed. Pizarro had feared the Incas would attack him and had suggested that both sides be unarmed when they met. Carelessly Atahualpa had agreed.

Pizarro's men had not forsaken their weapons; quite the reverse, they planned a surprise attack on the Incas if they thought they could get away with it. The Inca and his retinue squeezed into the square at Cajamarca, a densely packed mass, with no room to maneuver or run.

Pizarro gave the signal and gunners who had been hidden on the tops of the buildings around the square opened fire. With their war cry "Santiago," the Spanish cavalry in full armor and chain mail spurred their horses directly into the crowd of unarmed Indians, hacking and slashing with their broadswords. The result was panic and slaughter and one of the most lopsided battles in history. Within the space of two hours the Indians were annihilated. Thousands of Indians were killed, but not one of the Spanish lost his life or was seriously wounded in the attack. Most important from Pizarro's point of view, Atahualpa, the Lord Inca, had been captured. The supreme and total ruler of the empire was now in the hands of the invaders.

Atahualpa had completely and disastrously misunderstood the nature of the enemy he faced. As a captive he continued to underestimate the seriousness of his plight; he continued to be obsessed with the politics of the Inca civil war. His brother Huáscar was in the hands of his army, and even while in captivity Atahualpa was able to maintain a regular if clandestine contact with his forces. The army still obeyed the captive Inca without hesitation. Instead of uniting in a common cause with his brother and allowing him to go free in order to organize a national resistance to the Spanish invaders, Atahualpa secretly ordered Huáscar's execution, and he continued to order the killings of all members of Huáscar's faction. Twelve years earlier, Cortes had taken advantage of a civil war among the Aztecs in order to conquer Mexico. Pizarro was able to make even more dramatic use of the Inca civil war in his conquest of Peru.

Atahualpa realized that the Spanish were extremely greedy for gold, so he thought he would be able to buy them off. He took Pizarro into a room that measured twenty-two feet long by seventeen feet wide; he then pointed to a white line drawn about eight feet up on the wall and said that in two months he would fill the room with gold up to the line if the Spanish would then let him go. Pizarro was staggered and delighted by the prospect of so great a golden treasure falling into his hands without a struggle. He agreed at once. He also agreed to meet Atahualpa unarmed. As far as the Spanish were concerned, any agreement made between a Christian and an "enemy of God" was worthless.

Word went out to the farthest provinces of the Inca Empire that all the gold that could be obtained was to be sent immediately to ransom the Inca at Cajamarca. Temples and palaces were stripped of their golden ornaments, and caravans of thousands of llamas laden with gold were sent on their way to where the Inca was held captive. There is some dispute as to whether the terms of the ransom were ever completely fulfilled—certainly the gold arrived more slowly than Atahualpa had promised. There is some suspicion that Atahualpa's enemies in the civil war were holding back treasure. But a huge quantity of gold ultimately did arrive. Atahualpa's ransom was worth tens of millions of dollars by modern standards. No matter how much gold he got, however, Pizarro never had the slightest intention of releasing the Inca. There was a hasty and trumped up "trial." On July 26, 1533, Atahualpa, the Lord Inca was brought to the center of the square at Cajamarca and garroted. Over the next few months Pizarro also executed a number of the Inca's leading generals who had voluntarily surrendered in order to be with their emperor.

On November 15, 1533, Francisco Pizarro and his

little band of conquistadores triumphantly entered the Inca capital city of Cuzco. A mere handful of men had conquered a vast empire, almost without a fight.

This much of the history of the conquest of the Incas is well known. But the conquest did not end with the execution of Atahualpa and Pizarro's entry into Cuzco. It is with what happened later that this story is most concerned. After the initial shock, the Incas resisted their conquerors for half a century. They struck back at the Spanish from a part of their empire so remote, and from a city so well hidden, that its location was lost to history.

The province was called Vilcabamba; the city was called Vilcapampa or Vitcos. During the centuries in which the location of the city of Vilcapampa was lost, many legends grew up about it, and it proved to be so hard to find that people began to wonder whether it existed at all. Most of those who searched for Vilcapampa were lured on by tales of vast hidden treasures—the fabled "lost treasure of the Incas." The mystery of Vilcapampa attracted adventurers and treasure seekers from all over the world.

The man who finally penetrated the many mysteries of the realm of the last Incas was a young American named Hiram Bingham III. Bingham seems an unlikely sort of a discoverer, if only because he so nearly fulfills our fantasy of what an adventurer should be. The tale of his discovery reads as if it had been concocted in the script department of a major Hollywood studio. It seems the creation of Lucas and Spielberg, not authentic history. Bingham himself was like an actor who had been sent by central casting to play the part of the hero in this adventure fantasy. He started as the complete amateur, wandering through South America armed only with letters of introduction and a tourist guide, when he first succumbed to the lure of the lost city of the Incas. In the space of a few weeks he discovered not just one lost city but three. His discovery of Machu Picchu was and still is the most amazing archaeological find ever made in the Americas.

Bingham looked the part, too; he was tall, lean, handsome, rich, tough, brave, and unbelievably lucky. He faced one cliff-hanging danger after another without ever getting discouraged or turning back. Bingham really created our image of the explorer.

It is all too incredible—and it is all true.

But let's not get too far ahead of the story, for to understand the significance of Bingham's discoveries it is necessary to know more about the mysteries of Vilcapampa.

Basically the conquistador Francisco Pizarro was an illiterate and brutal thug, but he was no fool. He had cleverly used the hatreds of the Inca civil war in order to subdue the empire. He knew that he and his small band could never control an empire of millions once the shock of the capture and execution of the Inca wore off. Pizarro needed the help of the Incas themselves, and he decided that the best course of action was to appoint a puppet Inca—a member of the royal family, presumably from Huáscar's faction—who would be docile to Spanish control, yet still command the loyalty of the mass of Indians. Pizarro's first choice was Tupac Huallpa, a surviving younger brother of the defeated Huascar, who was no friend of the Atahualpa faction. But within three months Tupac Huallpa was dead—he may have been ill even before his sudden elevation to the position of Inca.

Pizarro now looked around for a new puppet and a candidate suddenly appeared—it was almost as if he had been sent from heaven. He was called Manco and was a son of Huayna Capac by a minor wife, a man with a slim but genuine claim to the position of Inca. Manco had been a fugitive from Atahualpa, and he arrived at the Spanish camp virtually alone and friendless, looking for protection just a few days after the death of Tupac Huallpa. Manco accompanied Pizarro to Cuzco and there was given the royal fringe—a woolen headpiece that was symbolic of imperial power among the Incas in the same way that the crown is symbolic of monarchical power in Europe. His title was Manco Inca, the same as that of the legendary founder of the Inca Empire. He is often called Manco II.

Like Atahualpa before him, Manco badly misjudged the character of the Spanish. He thought that they would help him consolidate his royal power and then they would go away, perhaps after the payment of some additional tribute. He soon learned that this was not to be. The Spanish were not going to go away, and instead of helping Manco regain his power, they intended to exercise all the power themselves. Manco was not to be a real ruler, merely a servant of Pizarro. Some of the Spanish even went out of their way to humiliate and insult the new Inca.

Nevertheless, Manco was not the only one to have made a miscalculation, for the Spanish had misjudged the character of their presumed puppet. By 1536, Manco decided that the only hope for the Incas lay not in cooperating with the invaders, but in driving them out of the Inca domain or killing them.

Manco Inca escaped from Cuzco and raised a great rebellion among the Indians, a rebellion that came very close to succeeding. Manco's troops besieged Cuzco and actually captured the great fortress of Sacsahuaman built above the city. Juan, one of Francisco Pizarro's three half brothers, was killed in the Spanish attempt to recapture the fortress.

The Spanish and their Indian allies held on and ultimately succeeded in breaking the siege and scattering Manco's great army. Manco always believed that he had hesitated just a bit too long before launching his attack on Cuzco and that had he attacked a few days sooner the city would have fallen to him. He may have been right, for he certainly came very close to victory.

Ultimately, however, a victory would have made little difference. Nor would there have been a major change in the course of history if Atahualpa had not trusted Pizarro but rather had ordered Pizarro and his little band ambushed and slaughtered the moment they entered Inca territory. As soon as the Spanish heard of the Incas, and of their gold, the empire of the Incas was doomed. The Spanish already had extensive settlements in the Americas, and they could call on the resources of their own homeland. There were lots of tough and ambitious young men in Spain who were looking for a way to make their fortune. The Incas, as a totally landbound people, never understood how the Spanish could get reinforcements from the sea.

If Cuzco had fallen to Manco, or if Pizarro and his men had been killed, there would have been others, and in the end the Spanish would have prevailed in Peru as they had in Mexico. Though the number of Spanish was tiny compared with the number of fighters that could be put into the field by the Incas, the Inca armies were no match for the conquistadores. Despite their remarkable accomplishments in engineering and organization, the Incas were still a technologically undeveloped people, particularly in warfare. They were much better farmers and builders than they were fighters.

The Spanish of the sixteenth century were probably the best fighters in the world. The most effective weapon the Incas possessed was a slingshot that could throw an egg-sized rock with great accuracy. The Spanish had gunpowder. They also had horses. Not only did the horses allow the Spanish to operate much more freely in the thin mountain air, the horses absolutely terrified the Indians and were probably more effective weapons than the guns. The Spanish had already conquered other Indian empires, and they knew what they were doing. The Incas, who had always lived in isolation from the rest of the world, had no experience with enemies of this sort; they simply did not know what had hit them.

Manco tried to adopt Spanish fighting techniques and was said to have appeared at the siege of Cuzco riding a captured horse. But after the failure of his great rebellion, Manco seemed to have realized that the Spanish could not be thrown out and that the only hope for the survival of the Incas (and for his own personal survival) was to get well beyond the reach of Pizarro and his troops.

The Inca gathered together his most loyal followers and offered them a choice. They could surrender to the Spanish and hope they would be able to strike some sort of deal with the new masters of Peru, or they could follow him into the jungle-covered mountains of Vilcabamba province, where he would establish a new Inca empire in a place where the Spanish could not reach them. Most chose to follow the Inca.

The Spanish did not want to have a resourceful and dangerous enemy like Manco Inca running around loose. They sent out several expeditions to destroy him and his remote headquarters. One of the expeditions was headed by Francisco Pizarro's youngest brother, Gonzalo. Once Gonzalo actually got close enough to Manco to hear the Inca shouting threats and insults at him from across a river, but as usual the Inca managed to slip away. The Spanish retired from the Vilcabamba region defeated and exhausted.,

Francisco Pizarro was so angered and frustrated by the failure to destroy Manco that he could respond only with savagery. He had captured Manco Inca's favorite wife. Now Pizarro had her horribly executed, and then he floated the mutilated body down a river where he was sure Manco's scouts would find it and bring it to their leader. That is what happened, and it only deepened Manco's hatred of the Spanish and of the Pizarros in particular.

The Spanish were beginning to have other problems. The conquistadores started squabbling among themselves over how the spoils of the rich land they had conquered would be split. Diego de Almagro, who had been Francisco Pizarro's partner in the original venture, had a falling out with the Pizarro brothers. In July 1538, Almagro was kidnapped and executed by the Pizarros. Three years later, the Almagrist faction retaliated by murdering the great Francisco Pizarro himself. Another Pizarro brother, Hernando, was imprisoned and sent back to Spain where he lived in luxurious but severely restricted exile. Gonzalo, the youngest of the four brothers, led an unsuccessful revolt in 1548 and was executed. Civil wars or what would more properly be described as gang warfare among the various factions ripped the former Inca Empire apart and so alarmed the king of Spain, the nominal ruler of Peru, that he sent his own officials directly from Spain to restore order to the land, which was rapidly swirling into anarchy.

Manco Inca watched all of this with great interest from his secret city. He had managed to establish a small but flourishing kingdom in Vilcabamba. The Incas supported themselves partly by agriculture, for as always they were superb farmers, and partly by boldly raiding Spanish settlements and caravans. Manco had learned the techniques of guerrilla warfare. The Inca still had hopes of regaining at least some of the power of his ancestors. Perhaps he dreamed of returning once again to Cuzco. He knew that he would never be able to strike a bargain with the Pizarros. That was because he had been responsible for the death of Juan Pizarro, who had been killed during the fighting at Cuzco in 1538.

Manco had always felt that he would have a better chance of working out an accommodation with Diego de Almagro. When Almagro was killed by the Pizarros, the Inca was very disappointed. When Francisco Pizarro was murdered by Almagrist supporters, Manco brightened considerably, and when seven Almagrists, including several who had actually participated in the murder of Pizarro, arrived in Vilcabamba on the run from the wrath of the Pizarro faction, Manco welcomed them. The seven fugitives promised to teach the Incas Spanish fighting techniques and to instruct them in the use of captured Spanish weapons. They also promised to intercede on Manco's behalf with the king of Spain, who had been none too pleased with the way the Pizarros had

been ruling Peru. The king, they said, might even restore Manco to his rightful capital.

Manco became very friendly with the fugitives, but
then something happened; it is not clear what, for while
there were several eyewitnesses to the event, the accounts differ considerably. It seems that Manco was
playing horseshoes with the seven Spanish fugitives
when one of them suddenly produced a knife and
stabbed the Inca repeatedly. Perhaps there had been an
argument over the game, or perhaps the assassin had
planned the attack for other reasons. No one knows. The
Spanish rushed off into the hills, but they got lost and
were captured by the Incas. Manco was mortally
wounded, yet he clung to life long enough to have the
satisfaction of knowing that the Spanish had been captured and tortured to death.

Thus ended the life of Manco Inca, the most persis-
tent and successful opponent the Spanish conquistadores
met anywhere in the Americas. Manco's death was
greatly mourned, not only in Vilcabamba where he had
ruled but throughout the former Inca domains, where
memory of Inca rule still commanded enormous affection
and loyalty among the Indians. Even the Spanish admitted that most of the Indians had supported Manco.
The Incas had been harsh masters to the common Indian, but the Spanish were far, far worse.

The death of Manco Inca did not end the story of the
Incas. Manco had established a flourishing kingdom in
Vilcabamba, and he had many sons who could assume
the power of the Lord Inca. The first to take the royal
fringe in Vilcabamba was Sayri-Tupac. However, he
was no warrior, and he longed to return to an easier life
in Cuzco, even if it meant life under the Spanish. Sayri-
Tupac opened negotiations with the Spanish and finally

led a group of his supporters out of Vilcabamba to Cuzco. A few months later Sayri-Tupac was dead. There was suspicion that he had been poisoned, either by the Spanish or by another faction of the Inca royal family that had already made its peace with the Spanish and may have feared that the famous Manco's son would somehow undermine their influence.

When Sayri-Tupac marched out of Vilcabamba, he did not do so as Lord Inca—he passed the royal fringe to another of Manco's sons, Titu Cusi. Titu Cusi was an interesting and complex character. In his youth he had lived among the Spanish, and he had been one of the witnesses to his father's murder. He was fond of showing visitors a scar on his leg that he said came from the knife slash of one of his father's killers.

The new Inca had a rather tolerant attitude toward the Spanish. He talked freely with their ambassadors, allowed some missionaries to enter his state and settle, and even had himself baptized. The baptism appears to have been primarily a political act, for Titu Cusi never paid any attention to the Christian religion; he was devoted to the old sun god of the Incas. While he was always polite to the Spanish, he was not about to be taken in by any promises, for he had seen such promises broken too many times. What Titu Cusi was trying to arrange was some sort of an agreement with the Spanish by which they would recognize the existence of an independent Inca state in Vilcabamba.

All of these plans ended abruptly in May 1571 when Titu Cusi died suddenly. The rumor spread that he had been poisoned by Father Diego Ortiz, one of the Spanish priests the Inca had allowed to settle in Vilcabamba. The new Inca, Tupac Amaru, yet another of Manco's sons, was swept up in a wave of anti-Spanish hatred, which the death of Titu Cusi had produced. Tupac Amaru tried to close the borders of Vilcabamba to all foreign influence, and he had Father Ortiz put to death.

Outside of Vilcabamba, Peru had changed dramatically. It was no longer in the control of the wild and warring conquistadores. The power was now in the hands of Francisco de Toledo, the viceroy from Spain, a coldly efficient man whose aim was to advance the interests of the Spanish crown at any and all costs. Toledo decided that Spain could no longer tolerate the existence of an independent Inca state. The death of Father Ortiz, who was instantly declared to be a holy martyr, gave him an excuse to launch a major military expedition against the last of the Incas.

Tupac Amaru was no Manco, and this time the Spanish succeeded. In June 1572, Spanish troops entered the city of Vilcapampa. Tupac Amaru escaped, but he had no taste for the life of a fugitive in the jungle, so he surrendered to the invaders. The Inca was sent back to Cuzco, where after undergoing a quick and probably forced conversion to Christianity he was executed in the city's main square. The shock and grief displayed by the thousands of Indians who had packed into the square alarmed the Spanish. The Inca's head had been cut off and was displayed on a pole, but it became an object of veneration for the Indians, and the Spanish were forced to take it down and bury it with the rest of his body.

Tupac Amaru was the last who could lay any real claim to the title of Inca. With his death the independent Inca state of Vilcabamba ceased to exist.

Vilcabamba had been something of an obsession for the Spanish since Manco had hidden himself there. But after Titu Cusi's death an extraordinary thing happened—people forgot where Vilcabamba had been. The city of Vilcapampa had supposedly been visited many times by Spanish ambassadors, fugitives, and priests, and had even been occupied by a Spanish army. Yet there existed no authentic record of where it was or what it looked like. The region was so wild and inaccessible that the Spanish never tried to settle the city themselves. Because of all the mystery the suspicion arose that the Spanish had never really seen the city of Vilcapampa and what they thought was Vilcapampa was really some other, less important city in Manco's domain, perhaps the city called Vitcos. Manco's real capital, it was rumored, was a sacred city that had never been shown to outsiders, and the secrets of the city died with the last Inca.

And there were other rumors, rumors of a great golden treasure to be found in the lost city. It was said that when Manco escaped from Cuzco he had taken much gold with him. Indeed, when Titu Cusi was captured he was found to have in his possession a famous golden image of the sun, for which the Spanish had been searching for many years. It was also said that even before Manco had come to Vilcabamba a great and mysterious city had existed there. And that the city of Vilcapampa was the original home of the Incas, and perhaps more ancient than the Inca Empire.

According to rumor a caravan of seven thousand llamas laden with gold for Atahualpa's ransom was passing through the province of Vilcabamba when word reached the caravan leaders that the Inca had been killed. Rather than let the gold fall into the hands of the Inca's murderers, they hid the treasure in the sacred and mysterious city of Vilcapampa. This was the most popular variation of the widely believed "lost gold of the Incas" tale that was told and retold in South America for hundreds of years. It was said that when Manco was forced to flee from the Spanish he retired to this hidden treasure city where he knew he would be safe.

So went the rumors. And for centuries adventurers hacked their way through the jungles and crawled up steep mountains searching for the lost city, the golden city of Vilcapampa. The searches were completely without success.

That is, until Hiram Bingham came into the picture.

CHAPTER 3

"The Bingham Blood"

Once, when thinking about his desire to run off to the wilds of Peru, Hiram Bingham said, "I feel the Bingham blood in my veins . . . as I start out for little known lands."

He may have been right, for the Binghams were an adventurous and surprising bunch—certainly not your average family next door.

The explorer's grandfather, the first Hiram Bingham, also became the first Protestant missionary in Hawaii way back in 1820. He was a lot more than a missionary, for by the sheer weight of his personality he became one of the most powerful, as well as one of the most hated, men in the islands.

A little over 150 years later, in 1971, the missionary's great-great-grandson Stephen allegedly smuggled a revolver into San Quenton Prison for prisoner and black activist George Jackson. Shortly thereafter, Jackson, two more inmates and three guards were killed in what was said to be a jailbreak attempt. It was one of the most violent and controversial episodes of a turbulent political era in America. Facing multiple counts of murder,

Stephen Bingham disappeared. His whereabouts are unknown to this day and remain one of the last great mysteries of that period.

In between these two vastly different figures is Hiram Bingham III—explorer, aviator, professor, and senator.

The Binghams have been in America for a long time. The first Bingham in America, Deacon Thomas Bingham, came over from England about 1650 and settled in Connecticut. The family has always had strong connections with that state, but they spread out all over New England. In the late eighteenth century, Calvin and Lydia Bingham were tending a modest farm in Bennington, Vermont. Most of Calvin and Lydia's six sons had already moved on to more fertile farms to the west or had abandoned farming entirely. Their son Hiram was supposedly destined to be the one to inherit the old family farm and to stay at home and take care of his aging parents.

But Hiram Bingham had other ideas. Since the days of Deacon Thomas, the Binghams had been a religious family, but Hiram took his religion even more seriously than the others. By the age of twenty-one, Hiram decided, much against the wishes of his family, that he was going to become a minister and a missionary. For the next eight years he received his ministerial training at a variety of schools, and for a time he studied with Reverend Elisha Yale, whose family had helped found Yale University. Bingham didn't have much money, but he was a dedicated and hard-working young man and thus was able to get by. He was ordained a Congregationalist minister in September 1819 and was ready to take on the challenging task of bringing Christianity to the distant Hawaiian Islands, or the Sandwich Islands, as they were more commonly called at that time. Bingham lacked only one thing a missionary needed—a wife. It was required that all missionaries be married in order to protect them from the "temptations" of life in strange environments.

As always Bingham was decisive. At his ordination he met Sybil Moseley, a deeply religious woman who also yearned for a missionary life. But women were forbidden to take part in the missionary crusade except as the wives of missionaries. A few days later Sybil and Hiram were married. On October 23, 1819, they boarded the brig *Thaddeus* in Boston harbor to begin the 18,000-mile voyage around the tip of South America to Hawaii. The five-month voyage was an absolute nightmare for the Binghams, who had never before left New England. They were crammed into a tiny cabin and were seasick most of the time. Yet when Hiram Bingham finally spied the lofty dormant volcano Mauna Kea of Hawaii on March 30, 1820, he said that he was ready to spring right off the boat and begin the great work of bringing the natives to Christ. His dedication and energy were overpowering, almost frightening. He never for a moment doubted the absolute rightness of his cause.

Hiram Bingham had arrived in Hawaii at a good time for missionaries. The Hawaiian Islands had had regular contact with ships from Europe and America since they were first reached by Captain Cook in the late eighteenth century. There was a small foreign community on the islands, but there had been no great missionary effort. However, the repeated contacts with Europeans and Americans had taken their toll on the Hawaiian people's established society and religion. Shortly before Bingham arrived, the old king had died, and his son was much less traditional and more open to foreign ideas, including Christianity.

Bingham made some early and influential converts among the Hawaiian nobility, and these converts encouraged, one might even say forced, their subjects into church and mission schools. Like most missionaries, Bingham had very severe and puritanical attitudes on such subjects as sex, gambling, and drinking. He used his influence among the chiefs to prohibit many activities that had made the Hawaiian Islands famous, even notorious, among sailors throughout the world. Bingham was not at all shy about denouncing everyone who disagreed with him as sinners and worse.

The sudden moral fervor that Hiram Bingham and his colleagues had inspired in Hawaii did not go down well with the sailors or indeed with the majority of foreign residents on the islands. One of the milder things Bingham was called was "a bleeding hypocrite." A businessman in Hawaii confided to his diary that he wished "Providence to put a whip in every honest hand [to] lash such rascals naked through the world." Others called the missionaries "blood suckers of the community." A Russian explorer who actually liked the Protestant Mission couldn't abide "Bengham" whose "religion is the cloak of all his designs." He called Bingham "an unenlightened enthusiast" who "meddles in all affairs of government . . . finding the avocations of ruler more to his taste than those of preacher."

Some sailors did not confine their objections to mere grumbling. In 1826 a mob of angry sailors from the *USS Dolphin* attacked Bingham's home, threatened his family, and might have injured or even killed the missionary if he had not been rescued by Hawaiian Christians. A year later a ship in the harbor lobbed cannonballs into the house where Bingham and his wife were staying.

Bingham was all for bringing Christianity to the islands, but he wanted his version of Christianity to prevail and would tolerate no rivals. During the 1830s he managed to have Catholic missionaries expelled from Hawaii and threatened that "blood would flow" if they ever returned. All of Bingham's activities were widely and favorably reported in the United States press. Whatever else he might have been, Hiram Bingham, Sr., was not the sort of man who could be easily overlooked.

Today missionaries of the Bingham sort are not popular, and his reputation has suffered greatly. Even by the end of his own life, his power and prestige on the islands had declined so sharply that when he was forced to leave the islands in 1840 because of his wife's illness, he was never able to return. There was no longer any place in the Hawaiian Islands for a single-minded missionary like Bingham. In James Michener's popular novel *Hawaii* the character of Abner Hale, the overbearing, bigoted, and generally villainous preacher, is clearly modeled on Hiram Bingham, Sr.

It might be expected that so formidable an individual would have considerable impact on his own children, and indeed he did, particularly on his oldest son, Hiram Bingham, Jr. From the moment of his birth on August 15, 1831, his father decided on his career. "Make him a good missionary," Bingham senior prayed.

Though Bingham junior was only nine when his family left the islands for good, he somehow always assumed that he would go back to take over his father's place as head of the Hawaiian mission. There was really nothing else in life that he desired to do. Bingham junior spent a lot of time with other Binghams in Connecticut, and when he came of age he attended Yale, where he allied himself with the more religiously active students in the school. After that he went to Andover Theological Seminary, the same school his father had attended.

While Bingham junior wanted only to follow in his father's footsteps, Bingham senior had far grander ideas for him. China had just been opened to Protestant missionaries, and Bingham senior saw the chance for his son to spread the Bingham brand of religion to the teeming millions of that vast nation. The thought of distant China absolutely terrified the young man. While never openly rebelling against his father's wishes, he did complain frequently to his sisters, and he pleaded with his father, but without much success.

While at Yale, Bingham junior had gained a sort of local fame for his athletic prowess—in fact, he was so good at sports and enjoyed them so much that his father began to worry lest this deflect him from his religious commitment. Once he was at Andover and the idea of going to China had become a real possibility, Bingham junior developed a bewildering series of ailments. His eyesight deteriorated, he had constant indigestion, and worst of all, chronic bronchitis affected his voice. A missionary without a strong voice was going to be severely handicapped. His afflictions actually caused him to leave Andover in 1856. China was now out of the question, and as soon as that was settled, Bingham junior's health improved wonderfully.

With his health restored, Bingham junior had to find a place where he might put his missionary training to use. China was out. For the time being, Hawaii wanted no more Binghams. So he set his sights upon another group of Pacific Islands that he thought would be quite similar to Hawaii, the Gilbert Islands. The missionary society was a bit dubious at first, fearing that Hiram junior might be as difficult and controversial a character as his father. Those who knew the young man assured the officials of the society that while his commitment was every bit as deep as his father's, his manners were much better.

There was only one thing left for Bingham junior to do before he began his life as a missionary; he needed to marry. He found a wife in Clara Brewster, a woman as devoted to Christianity as he was, and a good deal tougher, physically and mentally.

In 1857 the Binghams arrived in Honolulu aboard the *Morning Star*. It was to be a stopover on their way to the Gilbert Islands. Dramatic proof that not everyone in Hawaii had come to hate his father showed itself in the form of a crowd of Hawaiians chanting "Binama! Binama! Bingham! Bingham!" as they danced and swirled around the young missionary. They urged Bingham junior to stay in Hawaii and take the pulpit of his father's old church. He was sorely tempted. But he had made a commitment to bring the gospel to "those who had lived without it." So, rather than settle for the easy life in Hawaii, the Binghams reboarded the *Morning Star* to continue their voyage to the Gilbert Islands. They finally established their mission on the tiny coral island of Abaiang, which is in the northern part of the Gilberts, near the equator.

Bingham had expected a situation similar to the one that his father first found in Hawaii. But the reality was vastly different. The Gilberts were a small, obscure, and isolated chain of coral islands. One or at the most two ships a year stopped at Abaiang. Unlike the tropical paradise of Hawaii, the climate of the Gilberts was stifling and mostly dry year round. Moreover, the people showed no particular interest in adopting the new religion. Bingham persuaded the king to come to church once in a while, but the people did not follow him. In the first seven years of his mission in the Gilberts, Bingham made only four converts, and they were all eventually expelled for backsliding. Clara set up a school, but she never got more than ten students.

The whole mission had started badly. Just three months after their arrival Clara Bingham gave birth to a stillborn child. This plunged them both into despair from which they never really recovered. The food on Abaiang was limited and tasteless, the water was bad, and Bingham's health began to decline again. His letters to his family indicate that he was in a state of deep depression, yet he refused to give up and leave.

Ironically, this gentle but failed missionary inspired very different sentiments in the rare Western visitors than had his contentious (but successful) father. One visitor described Bingham junior as being "gentle, almost saintly." The writer Robert Louis Stevenson, who had no love of missionaries, passed through Abaiang and spoke of "the excellent Mr. Bingham" and his "golden memories." Bingham himself was more clear-sighted: "I felt grateful to him [Stevenson] for his words. I wish they had been better deserved."

Bingham junior decided that his lack of success and the general indifference that greeted other missionaries in the Gilberts were due in part to the fact that the people of the Gilbert Islands had no written language, and thus were unable to read the Bible for themselves. Bingham and his wife concluded that if they were not going to be able to convert the Gilbertese directly, the least they could do would be to give them a Bible they could read. And this meant virtually creating a written Gilbertese language. To this end they in effect locked themselves away for years to work on the project. They became hermits on the tiny island. By the end of 1864, Hiram and Clara decided that they had reached a point in their work where they would need to consult the proper Greek references on matters of style. Bingham felt he could now safely finish his work in Honolulu. More pressing was the fact that both he and Clara were so ill and worn down that had they stayed on Abaiang for another few months they probably would have died.

The Binghams spent most of the rest of their lives in Hawaii, with Hiram working on the Gilbertese Bible, which he finally finished in 1871. He also produced Bible commentaries written in Gilbertese, a Gilbertese-English dictionary, and a host of other works in the Gilbertese language. Clara assembled Bible stories for Gilbertese children, a geography, an arithmetic primer, and much more. Between them the Binghams produced the entire written literature of the Gilbertese people. But only once, briefly and very nearly fatally, did they ever return to the Gilbert Islands. In 1873 the Binghams decided to once again try missionary work on Abaiang. A few months after his arrival on the island Bingham became ill, and the longer he stayed the sicker he got. To complicate matters, Clara was now pregnant. After her first stillborn child there were many years in which Clara either could not or would not become pregnant. Now she was going to have a baby, and they were stuck on the hated Abaiang, which held so many grim memories.

On May 16, 1875, the Binghams managed to get a ship that took them out of the Gilberts. It sailed in a leisurely way from Samoa to Fiji to New Zealand. At every port the suffering Hiram Bingham had to be carried off, and he would have to be nursed back to enough health to survive the voyage to the next port. Finally the miserable couple were able to catch a steamer back to Hawaii, and they arrived in port just six days before their son, Hiram III, was born. So in this rather dramatic fashion the future explorer, professor, aviator, and senator entered the world on November 19, 1875.

In his sense of mission and steely determination to persevere no matter what the obstacles, and in his physical toughness (for Hiram junior had been an excellent athlete in his youth), Hiram III resembled his father and grandfather. But in most other ways he broke completely with the established family traditions. It's not hard to understand why he did this, and how.

Hiram III's father was nowhere near the formidable character that his grandfather had been. Besides, when the boy was born his parents were both in their forties, exhausted and often bedridden for much of their son's childhood. The household also consisted of several Bingham aunts who were even older than his parents. Said Clara Bingham, the family consisted of "quiet, almost worn-out people." The household was a gloomy sort of a place, preoccupied with illness, death, and preparation for death. However, neither of Bingham's parents nor his aunts died during his childhood, though they constantly talked of their impending deaths. In fact, his father lived on until 1908, and then his death came as a surprise.

Hiram junior called his home Gilbertinia, in honor of those islands to which he had devoted so much of his life and which he must have hated so passionately, even if he could never admit it. The house was located on a tract of land that had been given to Hiram senior by the Hawaiian king he had helped to convert. So Hiram III grew up surrounded with reminders of his family's past power and glory in the islands.

Years later when Bingham became an explorer and

was planning to climb mountains in South America, he recalled mountain climbing in Hawaii with his father when he was only four years old. But given the condition of his father's health, mountain climbing couldn't have been a very common activity, if indeed it ever happened at all. The Binghams seemed primarily to be concerned about keeping their son away from the distractions of worldly entanglements. And that wasn't easy.

In the old days when Hiram senior set the moral tone for the islands, or at least for the missionary families, dancing and cardplaying were not allowed and no missionary's son was ever supposed to consider a secular career. In half a century Hawaii had changed. Even the sons of missionaries were seen dancing and playing cards, and when they got old enough, most of them left the missionary fold for the attractions of wealth and a secular life in the increasingly wealthy and secular islands.

Hiram III wasn't safe from contact with such influences even in the mission school he attended. Hiram junior constantly reminded his son that he was a Bingham and he had a tradition to uphold. The boy was often isolated from other children and very lonely. What Hiram junior failed to recall is that Hiram senior had once been destined by his parents to become a farmer, but Hiram senior had rebelled and had taken off to pursue his own life in a distant land.

Hiram III's rebellion began rather modestly in a public library. In the Bingham family the reading of novels was considered a frivolous and possibly even dangerous waste of time. Nevertheless, occasionally on Saturdays the young man would sneak off to the Honolulu public library, hide himself in a remote corner, and indulge in such forbidden pleasures as Mark Twain's

Huckleberry Finn. Like Huck, Hiram III dreamed of a freer life away from his moralistic family.

Of course, in Hawaii you couldn't just build a raft and set off down the river. Hiram III did the next best thing. When he was twelve he withdrew money from the bank account that was set aside for his education and tried to book passage on a steamer to San Francisco. He didn't get away with it, but the attempt shocked his family, and they wondered if, perhaps, they were keeping the boy in too restrictive an environment.

The young man had been reading more than Mark Twain. He had also encountered the rags-to-riches sagas of Horatio Alger. This inspired him with "dreams of rising from newsboy to wealthy philanthropist." Bingham wasn't quite in the position of Alger's ragged newsboys and bootblacks, but his family was by no means wealthy. They lived off the none too generous largesse of the missionary society that had employed Hiram senior and junior. Since the missionary effort was in decline, they kept cutting the Binghams' stipend. The Binghams had some Hawaiian property, acquired in the days of Bingham senior's power, and they still had some influential friends in Hawaii and influential friends and relatives back in the States. Still, the Binghams always considered themselves poor, and that was the way they wanted it. Father always used to tell his son that it was no shame to be "the son of a poor man." Both Bingham senior and junior had been relatively indifferent to wealth, and Bingham junior was almost hostile to it. Both had tried to protect "their natives" from the encroachments of Western wealth and the material values it brought. They tried to inculcate their children with the same attitude toward wealth; with Hiram III the lesson didn't seem to take.

What with an elderly and rather gloomy household,

isolation from the majority of the community around him, and restrictions that he found increasingly difficult to obey, Hiram Bingham III's childhood was not an especially happy one. Yet as everyone said, his parents were good people at heart, and his relationship with them was an affectionate if increasingly distant one. Moreover, Bingham always loved Hawaii itself. Later in his life when he was to explore some of the most spectacular scenery in the world, the highest compliment he could pay to anything he saw was to compare it favorably with scenes from his Hawaiian childhood.

In 1892 when Hiram III was fourteen his parents returned to the United States to oversee the publication of the Gilbertese Bible. When they left to return to Hawaii, Hiram III remained behind to continue his schooling at Phillips Academy in Andover, Massachusetts.

When the young man entered Phillips he was already quite tall for his age and very good-looking. He also possessed a natural, easy charm, not at all the sort of personality one would think would develop in a family as isolated and unworldly as the Bingham family. Hiram III was very different from his father and grandfather, and those differences were to become ever more apparent over the next few years.

It's possible that the elder Binghams had led such isolated lives that they had not realized how different the world was from what they imagined it to be and how much it had changed since 1819 when Hiram senior first set sail for Hawaii. Certainly they did not realize how much Phillips Academy had changed. It had once been almost exclusively a religious school connected to the Andover Theological Seminary. Phillips had evolved into a school where there were more courses in the sci-

ences and humanities than in religion, and students discussed current events, not the Bible. It had become, in
short, a worldly establishment, just the sort of place the
Binghams had tried to protect their son from.

Still, at first the school seemed to be having a good
effect on young Hiram as far as his parents were concerned. His letters were filled with regret for his earlier
disobedience. And they also contained the startling an-
nouncement that he was no longer interested in making
money. He singled out the case of Jay Gould, the notorious robber baron who was much in the news at that time.
"Look at Jay Gould . . . what a record. The papers tell
how many millions he amassed and in the next line tell
about the men he *ruined* to get the money." The young
man was, after all, only fourteen, and he was away from
home for the first time. He was homesick and a bit frightened by the new world in which he found himself. Soon
he adjusted to his new life and his self-confidence came
back.

At the Phillips Academy of the 1890s sports rivaled
religion for the passionate devotion of students. Some
students actually attended Sunday services in their athletic uniforms, an act which would have been unthink-
able to earlier Binghams. Hiram III became deeply involved in sports, not so much as a player but as a
businessman. Since he was not a rich man's son, he was
always in need of money. He managed the football team
and ran the food concession, and was able to turn a nice
profit in these enterprises. During the summer he sold
books, often using the family's religious connections as
an introduction to possible customers.

There was nothing disreputable or dishonest about
any of his activities, but such activities were so utterly

alien to his family that every letter he sent them seemed to contain a new shock or disappointment. For his part, Hiram III came to dread the weekly letter from home, admonishing him gently but regretfully for slipping into worldly ways. Later Bingham was to write to his father, "We live in two different worlds of thought and my philosophy does not seem good to you because it has been born and nurtured under different conditions."

Hiram III had certainly not abandoned religion, and when he entered Yale in the fall of 1894 his father entertained hopes that he would yet become a missionary. After all, *he* had attended Yale, and Hiram senior had actually studied religion under one of the Yales. The boy could still be saved. What the elder Bingham did not understand was that Yale too had changed dramatically since he had attended, and the time that Hiram III spent there marked his further estrangement from the missionary world of his father and grandfather.

At Yale the young man developed a sense of fashion and social status, concepts utterly alien to other members of his family. He quickly joined as many of the powerful student organizations as he could. Though he was, as his father had so often reminded him, the son of a poor man, Hiram III had the charm and the poise to move easily and comfortably among his wealthier fellow students.

He took up smoking a pipe, because all Yale men smoked a pipe. "It looks well," he told his horrified parents. He took up playing cards ("99 percent of the fellows in College—if not more—do it"), he regularly attended dances, and he read popular novels. All of these activities Hiram senior had tried to have banned from Hawaii when he had the power to do so. When old-fashioned evangelical preachers, the kind that had inspired his father and grandfather, visited the campus, young Bingham and his friends were very cool and privately derided the preachers as "cranks."

The fondest hope of the Binghams was that their only son would become a medical missionary and fulfill his father's thwarted plan to go to China. During his years in New England young Bingham had been far more impressed by the secular teachers he had met than by the ministers. So he finally and firmly informed his parents that he was not going to be a missionary but a teacher, because "no minister has one-fifth of the chance to accomplish more good and affect the world more by his influence than a teacher."

The elder Binghams were driven to near despair by their only child's apparent surrender to the secular modern world. They were totally at a loss as to how to handle the matter. The first two Hiram Binghams had chosen their wives in order to fulfill their missionary duties. The handsome and popular Hiram III just seemed to enjoy the company of young women. When the young man sent his parents a letter describing how much fun he had had at a Christmas dance, he was answered with a pile of religious tracts denouncing the evils of dancing. When he said he had a girlfriend, he was warned against "worldly entanglements," and when one of his girlfriends turned out to be a Christian Scientist, his parents were nearly frantic. They practically told him that he would go to hell if he got mixed up with such a woman.

In 1898 Bingham's parents, after years of ineffectually trying to change their son's ways, suddenly found hope that he might return to the missionary fold. Bingham was a joiner who had kept his connections with student religious movements, and he was sent as a delegate to an international student religious conference in

Cleveland. Surrounded by religious enthusiasm young Bingham was swept up by it so suddenly and completely that he wrote "I seem . . . to be approaching insanity." He gave the money he had saved for his education to the missionary cause, and applied for and was accepted as a missionary at Palama Chapel in Honolulu, Hawaii. He could even live at home.

His parents were surprised but naturally delighted. They felt that once he was home, he might eventually decide to fulfill the long-held family dream of a mission in China. It was not to be, because Hiram III's religious revival was short-lived. Once he was home he tried to fall into the regular routine of religious observances, which he had rebelled against when he was a child. He found that he was no more comfortable with them now than he had been before he went to New England. He began to argue theology with his father, and soon he resigned his position at the Honolulu chapel because he felt that he could no longer teach the sort of orthodox religion that was required of him. His brief return to the missionary fold was over.

Bingham's decision to break with the family missionary tradition was not an easy one. When he had returned to Hawaii and taken up his duties at Palama Chapel, his health began to suffer. His eyesight failed and his lungs gave out, so that he could no longer sing or even talk loudly without being racked by coughing. These were the exact symptoms that his father had suffered when he had faced the prospect of going to China many years before. When Bingham left Honolulu to take a job as a chemist on a sugar plantation, his health improved immediately. In a rare unkind moment his father wrote that the ill health might be an "excuse" for withdrawing from missionary work.

Bingham had another reason for abandoning the missionary life at that moment. While he had been mixing with the rich and fashionable in New England he had met a young woman named Alfreda Mitchell. She was the very wealthy heir to the Tiffany fortune. In 1898 while Bingham was working at the chapel, the Mitchell family came to Honolulu as part of a world cruise, and the two young people met again. Their relationship blossomed rapidly. They announced their intention of getting married, a decision that pleased neither family.

As far as the Binghams were concerned, the Mitchells were just the sort of worldly folk that they had spent their entire life fighting. They thought that their son would be seduced by wealth and social status and that he would lose his soul. The Mitchells were not overjoyed at the prospect of their daughter's marrying a poor and unemployed, though good-looking and charming, son of a missionary.

The Mitchells' reservations highlighted a very real problem for Hiram Bingham. Since he had abandoned his brief fling with a missionary life he was a man without a career. The Mitchells encouraged him to go back to school and get an advanced degree so that he could get a respectable academic position. They did more than encourage him; they said they would not allow their daughter to announce her engagement until he did so.

So Hiram Bingham III was now committed to becoming a college teacher. He didn't even bother to go as far as the old family stamping ground of New England and Yale, but instead went directly to California and enrolled in history at the University of California at Berkeley. This was a final blow to his father. His son was going to a school filled with people who didn't even have a nodding acquaintance with the family religion. "No good can come from such an unholy alliance," he groaned.

When Bingham set out to write his master's thesis he chose a subject he knew well, the rise of American influence in Hawaii. He fully recognized that missionaries like his grandfather were now out of fashion. He defended them as characters in a "heroic mould." But he also acknowledged that they were human and had made many mistakes and that their "extreme puritanical views" had probably damaged the Hawaiian people.

Bingham's break with his missionary past was now complete. He had started an entirely new phase of his life. At this point he thought of himself as a teacher—but that wasn't to last long, and very soon Hiram Bingham III was to take up the title of explorer.

CHAPTER 4

The Wandering Scholar

O n November 20, 1900, Hiram Bingham III took a vital step toward becoming an explorer. He got married. At first glance that may not seem like a vital step, but consider the practical problems involved in running off to look for lost cities and unknown lands. Exploring costs a lot of money, and back in the early years of the twentieth century only the wealthy and the well connected could afford the luxury of taking a few years off to live in primitive conditions and risk their lives in the pursuit of the unknown. Exploring was very much a gentleman's occupation, and with his marriage Bingham was catapulted from being a poor missionary's son to being a wealthy gentleman.

Bingham was marrying Alfreda Mitchell, the granddaughter of Charles Lewis Tiffany, the immensely successful jeweler, merchant, and swordmaker. The wedding, held at the Mitchell estate in New London, Connecticut, was supposed to be a quiet affair. However, it attracted the rich and the prominent from many walks of life. There were academics and artists and politicians as well as businessmen.

Bingham had kept his part of his bargain with the Mitchell family and energetically pursued his academic career. Shortly before his marriage he had received his master's degree from the University of California, and he became a doctoral candidate in South American history at Harvard University. Though Bingham had no prior interest in, or connection with, South America, it seemed a wide-open and promising field for an ambitious young scholar. The United States was taking a new interest in Central and South America, and there was a need for scholars.

Bingham was bright and enthusiastic, and academic success came easily to him. By 1905 he had obtained his doctorate and a good position at Princeton University in New Jersey. The Bingham family began to grow, with Amanda having sons at the rate of almost one a year. Ultimately they had seven sons. Hiram Bingham now seemed to have everything that he had once dreamed of as a boy huddled in a corner of the reading room of the Honolulu Public Library.

But in truth Hiram Bingham wasn't very happy or satisfied. The restrictions of the academic life and of his new-found social status and ever-growing family began to weigh heavily on him, just as the restrictions of Gilbertinia once had. While Bingham had everything that he had once wanted out of life, he now wanted more. He wanted to be famous and he wanted to be free. As he worked his way through one dusty volume of South American history after another, Bingham began to formulate a plan that he hoped would gain him both fame and freedom.

In the early years of the twentieth century there were two ways of looking at history. In one view individuals counted for very little, and history was moved by broad underlying conditions such as economics, climate, and religion. The other view held that history was really changed by the actions of certain great men. In this view, if men like Alexander the Great or Napoleon had not existed, the course of history would have been vastly different. Hiram Bingham, who always had been attracted by tales of heroes and heroic actions, was a firm believer in the great man theory of history. He thought that the lives of such men should not only be studied but also emulated.

Bingham's heroes in South American history were the liberators Simón Bolívar and José de San Martín. These famous soldier-statesmen had led the fight to free the nations of South America from Spanish rule in the early nineteenth century. Both were dashing and romantic figures who showed not only great political skill and military talent but great personal bravery and style as well. They didn't just sit back and make strategy, they rode at the head of their troops enduring hardship and facing danger during their difficult campaigns. They were men of strong emotions and great passion. They were, in short, heroes. As far as Hiram Bingham was concerned, these were the sort of people who shaped history. Their lives were what history was all about. It wasn't poring over books and manuscripts, and it wasn't lecturing to a roomful of uninterested students.

Bingham proposed that he should write a massive work on the campaigns of Bolívar. But in order to write a book on such a man he couldn't just sit in a library in New England copying what others had written—he had to go where Bolívar had gone, see what he saw. In a sense he had to experience what Bolivar had experienced. Bingham proposed to retrace "the route of his most celebrated campaigns" and visit the site of all the important battles. It was to be an epic work that would make his career as a scholar. At least that was what he told people.

Bingham took this ambitious plan to his wealthy Tiffany relatives and asked them if they would finance his travels through South America. They agreed quickly, for the sort of exploration Bingham proposed was considered to be a proper gentlemanly occupation, and a successful biography of Simón Bolívar would certainly add to the young scholar's standing in the academic world.

Later in life Bingham tried to play down the romance and sheer love of adventure that he brought to his travels. He insisted that all his expeditions were well planned and he always had some high scientific or scholarly purpose in mind. That was a fiction that he was never really able to carry off very well. For he was the very picture of the adventurer on the run from the restrictions of ordinary life. There was still a lot of Huck Finn in him, but he was going a lot farther than the Mississippi River.

On this the first of his South American expeditions Bingham set off on muleback across vast and unpopulated regions of Colombia and Venezuela. Unaccountably, he traveled during the rainy season, so he spent a lot of time forcing his reluctant mule across flood-swollen rivers. At other points he cut his way through tropical jungles with a machete and crossed snow-choked mountain passes. Once his expedition lost all of its supplies, and Bingham had to spend hours up to his waist in water in a dangerous swamp, hunting for food. He was also accused of being an American spy and was "bitten by 7,238,961 insects." The supposedly well-planned expedition could easily have resulted in disaster for the young scholar.

In the end, though he talked about it a lot, Bingham never did write his Bolívar biography. But he had found what he really wanted to do in life. Despite all the hardships and dangers and near disasters, Hiram Bingham loved every minute of his travels. He reveled in his ability to face and overcome the dangers of exploration. He was out of the classroom, out of the library, and though he never said it in so many words, he was away from his growing family. He was meeting what President Theodore Roosevelt called "the stern test of actual life."

As soon as Bingham returned from South America he began looking around for some way to go again. An excuse was soon found: the First Pan-American Scientific Congress to be held at Santiago, Chile, at the end of December 1908 and the beginning of January 1909. U.S. Secretary of State Elihu Root heard of Bingham's first trip and discussed it with him. Root liked the young man, and through the secretary of state Bingham managed to get himself appointed as a delegate from the United States, even though he was certainly no scientist and he didn't have a very clear notion of what he was supposed to do at the congress.

In 1906 he said he was going to trace Bolívar's route. This time he decided that in addition to going to Santiago he would follow what he called "the most historic highway in South America," the old trade route between Lima, Potosí, and Buenos Aires. It was a road that was "used by the Incas and their conqueror Pizarro; by Spanish viceroys, mine owners, and merchants; by the liberating armies of Argentina; and finally by Bolívar and Sucre, who marched and countermarched over it in the last campaigns of the Wars of Independence."

Bingham started his trip in a most leisurely fashion. He took a boat to England and then recrossed the Atlantic, landing in Brazil. In 1908 direct sailings from New York to South America were not frequent, and the American ships were less comfortable than the typical English or continental vessel. Bingham contrived to miss the American ship. "Personally I was glad of the excuse to go the longer way, for I knew that the exceedingly comfortable new steamers of the Royal Mail Line were likely to carry many Brazilians and Argentinos, from whom I could learn much that I wanted to know."

Bingham had deliberately chosen a ship that made its way very slowly down the east coast of South America, so that he could stop and visit as many port cities as possible. The young scholar wandered about, much as any other tourist. At this point he was not so much interested in history as he was in the present and future of the places he visited. In Pernambuco he found that the bustling customs house "gives promise of a larger and more important city in the years to come, when the new docks shall have been built and still more modern methods introduced."

This was another indication of just how far removed his ideas now were from those of his missionary grandfather and particularly from those of his father. They lived by the missionary creed, which was "to anticipate and counteract the invasions and corruptions of commerce by introducing . . . the purifying influence of the Gospel, in advance of an infidel, corrupting civilization."

Hiram Bingham III could see nothing but good coming from the advance of civilization.

It wasn't until Bingham got out of the cities and beyond the reach of the railway that his trip really began. In November, Bingham had gotten as far as Buenos Aires. At that point he decided to strike out into the interior and visit the legendary mining city of Potosí. On this part of the journey Bingham was accompanied by another gentleman adventurer, Huntington Smith, Jr., a fellow Yalie. They could have gone to Potosí via stagecoach: "But we had enough of being shaken to pieces in a stage-coach, and decided we could see the country better and be more independent if we used saddle mules." Bingham was so tall that when mounted on a mule his legs dangled perilously close to the ground. Yet he always enjoyed that particular mode of travel above all others.

The journey to Potosí was not without danger, as travelers often fell prey to bandits who roamed the Bolivian highlands. In fact, before they started their journey Bingham and Smith actually met some of the most notorious bandits, though at first they didn't know it. In the town of La Quiaca, Argentina, near the Bolivian border, they fell in with a couple of rough-looking Americans. The men entertained Bingham and Smith with hair-raising tales of the robbers who lived on the Bolivian roads. The worst of these robbers, they said, were criminals who had been driven out of America, but had found a home in the lawless highlands of Bolivia. It was only after a long conversation that the two Americans told Bingham and Smith that they were the gang leaders. They had probably decided to find out more about the travelers, to see if they were detectives from the States, and if they weren't, to see if they had anything worth stealing. The robbers apparently decided that Bingham and Smith represented no danger and had nothing worth stealing, for they were never bothered.

The robbers insisted that their profession was an honorable one and that they would not harm anyone who did not set out to harm them. Nor were they interested in troubling solitary travelers. Their business, they said, consisted of attacking armed payroll stages loaded with cash going to the mines. This they felt was perfectly legitimate plunder taken in a fair fight.

"Having laid this down for our edification, [the robbers] proceeded to tell us what a reckless lot they were and how famous had been their crimes, at the same time assuring us that they were all very decent fellows and quite pleasant companions." Bingham was not totally reassured and was quite happy never to have to meet this particular group of Americans again.

As Bingham bounced on muleback into the Bolivian highlands, he was entering territory that in a short time would become very important to him, though he certainly was not aware of this at that moment. He was entering territory that had once been on the frontier of the great Inca empire.

This was also the first time that Bingham came into extended contact with the Quechuas, those Indians who had once been the subjects of the Incas. Indeed, the Incas were not outsiders, but were the royal family of one group of Quechuas. The ordinary Quechuas had been oppressed by the Incas and even more brutally oppressed by the Spanish conquerors. Wrote Bingham, "From the earliest historical times these poor Indians have virtually been slaves." They were poverty stricken, usually undernourished, and addicted to chewing on cotic coca leaves, which dulled the pangs of hunger and the pain of overexertion at high altitude.

In his travels, Bingham witnessed repeated examples of brutality toward the Quechuas. At the town of Escara, Bingham saw a Bolivian officer become enraged at his Quechua guide who he thought was moving too slowly. The officer suddenly lost his temper and began beating the unresisting guide with his riding whip. "The Indian stood for a few moments, and then commenced to back off, followed by the officer who continued to lay on the blows as fast as possible." Though he made no move to help the man who was being beaten, Bingham found this "a sickening sight." What Bingham found most surprising was the Indian's inability to fight back or resist in any way. Ultimately what he regarded as the Quechuas extreme passivity came to irritate him.

Hiram Bingham was by no means a cruel man. Unlike many Americans of his day he genuinely enjoyed people of other races and cultures. But he was also a man of his times, and today his attitude toward the "natives," Quechua or otherwise, would seem unenlightened, patronizing, even bigoted. But it is misleading to judge the attitudes of 1909 through the insights of the 1980s. In most respects Bingham's racial and cultural attitudes would have to be considered advanced for his day. Bingham believed that a long history of virtual slavery and a combination of malnutrition and cocaine addiction had made the Quechuas passive.

Bingham found the Bolivian highlands bleak and monotonous, and he wondered how it was possible to scratch even a bare subsistence living out of such an uncompromising landscape. The journey was, at best, an uncomfortable one. Bingham and Smith went from one poste, or posthouse, to the next. These collections of mud huts dominated his thoughts. They were located about every fifteen or twenty miles along well-traveled roads. At the poste the traveler, if he was lucky, could get alfalfa for his mule and perhaps some food for himself (a highly spiced and barely edible llama stew was the most common fare) and a place on the floor to sleep. Nights in the Bolivian highlands were cold, windy, and often wet. At first Bingham found all these postes "more or less dirty and uncomfortable," but after a few days of travel he changed his mind and thought of them as "a perfect haven of rest."

Sometimes there was no food for man or mule, and no place to sleep, but one could always demand and receive some hot water for tea. Bingham noticed that people always drank tea or something stronger, never cold water. Indeed, he was warned specifically against drinking cold water at high altitudes. But at one spot he was attracted by a crystal clear waterfall, and since the day had been hot and he was thirsty, he decided to have a drink. A Bolivian who had joined up with the Americans told Bingham not to do it, but Bingham brushed aside the objection, saying that he had a strong constitution and a little drink of water wouldn't hurt him. In fact, Bingham did have a strong constitution. He traveled everywhere and ate and drank anything, usually without suffering any ill effects. But this time he had made a mistake.

In about an hour he began to feel chilly. "Hot tea followed by hot soup and still hotter brandy and water failed to warm me. . . ." He became so dizzy that he couldn't stand, and so he stretched out on the warm stones in front of the poste. Nausea, vomiting, and diarrhea followed, and Bingham knew that he had mountain sickness. The symptoms were bad enough; what was even worse from Bingham's point of view was the prospect of being violently ill and stuck in a wretched little poste at least twenty miles from the nearest doctor, who was located in the city of Potosí. Bingham determined that he was going to get back on his mule and that no matter how sick he was he would not get off until he reached Potosí.

Upon leaving the poste Bingham had to pay the bill. As he reached into his wallet for his last piece of paper currency, Bingham's hand was trembling so badly from the chills that he tore the bill, and the proprietor refused to accept a torn bill. Bingham didn't have any other small bills; the proprietor didn't have any change. Bingham was at a loss to know what to do. There was an argument. Sick and exasperated, Bingham finally just shoved the man up against the wall, staggered out to his mule, and rode off. It was, he admitted, a "lawless performance," but Hiram Bingham was not feeling very patient at that moment. The twenty-mile ride across the plateau in the face of an icy wind was one of the low points of Bingham's career as an explorer.

At Potosí the travelers were lucky enough to find a hotel. Bingham was literally carried upstairs to a second-floor bedroom, and a doctor who was thoroughly experienced in treating mountain sickness was summoned. Bingham's understated comment was, "I felt quite willing to retire from active exploration for a day or two."

Mountain sickness is one of those ailments that first makes you fear you are going to die and then, as the pain grows worse, makes you fear you won't. But it only rarely leaves lasting aftereffects, and in a couple of days Bingham was back on his feet, taking an active interest in his surroundings, and they were interesting indeed. Potosí, he decided, was the most fascinating city in South America.

Potosí has a brilliant and ghastly history, yet it is virtually unknown in the United States. In the middle of the sixteenth century, just about the time the major gold mines of South America had been exhausted, silver was discovered at Cerro Potosí, a hill rising about 1,500 feet above the city. The hill turned out to be the richest single source of silver ever discovered. Said Bingham, "No tale of the Arabian Nights, no dream of Midas, ever equalled the riches that flowed from that romantic [hill]." But at what cost.

The Potosí mine is located some fifteen thousand feet above sea level. Silver mining under any conditions is a hazardous occupation, but at that altitude prolonged work in the mines is fatal. Bingham found that just crawling in and out of one of the mines was exhausting. The climate of Potosí is damp and cold year round. The Spanish conquistadores forced Indians to work in the mines under conditions that were so horrible that the authorities back in Spain were shocked and alarmed. There were numerous decrees passed requiring the humane treatment of the workers (who in reality were more like slaves), but these decrees did little to ease the plight of the Indians, for whom transportation to the mines was equal to a death sentence. It has been estimated that more Indians died in the mines than in the conquest itself and all of the revolts and civil wars that followed.

At the beginning of the seventeenth century when cities like New York and Boston barely existed, Potosí, despite its frightful climate, was a large and extremely wealthy city, and for over a century it was the largest city in the Western Hemisphere, and incomparably the wealthiest. The roads that ran to it were the busiest thoroughfares in the Americas.

In the days of its extravagant glory, sumptuously clad grandees rode their beautifully decorated horses up and down the narrow stony streets, bowing to ladies dressed in the most expensive clothes that their newfound wealth could buy. Just outside the city, thousands of wretched miners starved and died to create this wealth. Perhaps nowhere in history have the contrasts between rulers and ruled been more starkly on display.

Potosí's wealth was based entirely on the silver mines, and when the silver gave out, as it inevitably did, the city began to crumble. When Bingham visited Potosí, the population had fallen from a high point of 160,000 to a bare 15,000. It was in many respects a city of ruins.

On the outskirts were abandoned ore smelters and the remains of the buildings in which the thousands of miners had lived and died. The city once had at least sixty churches, but Bingham found that at least half of them had crumbled away, and even so, they were better preserved than the mansions and other fine buildings that had been built on the orders of the newly wealthy mine owners.

As soon as Bingham was back on his feet again, he began wandering about the city, fascinated by its churches, mines, and jam-packed marketplaces. There were no carriages and few horses in Potosí, but there were plenty of llamas in the streets. These animals never failed to amuse Bingham. He said they reminded him of some of the society people that he knew. Bingham was also struck by the Cerro itself, a beautifully colored hill that was honeycombed with mining tunnels.

In his wanderings Bingham made the mistake of

walking into the backyard of his hotel, where the meals he ate were prepared. The filth he found "indescribable," and he wondered why he didn't get "every disease in the calendar." But he didn't.

In the days of its glory Potosí had attracted thousands, but as Bingham noted, "the dreadful climate, the high altitude, the cold winds and the chilling rains drove away those who could afford it to the more hospitable valleys." In the valley lay Sucre, a city that was wealthier and in many respects more influential than La Paz, the capital of Bolivia. Though he could have gone to Sucre by stagecoach, Bingham, as usual, chose to make the journey by mule.

The wealthiest people in Bolivia lived in Sucre, and a good deal had been spent on beautification of the city, yet Bingham didn't like it at all. The hotel proprietor kept spitting on the carpet, the bank gave him counterfeit coins, and worst of all, people made fun of him when he went out. "Whenever we walked the streets examining the public buildings or visiting the market place we were considerably annoyed by loafers both men and boys, who recognizing us as strangers and foreigners regarded us as the proper target for all manner of witticisms." They made fun of the way he dressed, and that was something the image-conscious Hiram Bingham simply could not stand. "We were not sorry when the time came to leave Sucre," he huffed.

As Bingham and his companion pushed onward, they left the land of the Quechuas and entered the territory of the Aymaras. If Bingham found the Quechuas too passive, the Aymaras were another matter entirely; they were vigorous and rather brutal. At Aymara postes the travelers were treated insolently, and at Aymara towns the hostility of these Indians toward the Americans was so great that Bingham felt that he might really be in danger. While wandering the streets of the Aymara town of Oruro, Bingham found himself amid a group of drunken miners. "Certain parts of Oruro are not pleasant places in which to take a walk. In fact, I never felt more uncomfortable in my life."

At Oruro, Bingham was forced to abandon his mules and once again enter the world of trains and timetables. And thus by slow stages and roundabout routes Bingham finally approached the city of Santiago, Chile, site of the First Pan-American Scientific Congress to which he was a delegate.

For the record the main purpose of his trip was to attend the congress, but for Bingham it was an anti-climax, almost an unwelcome interruption in his travels. "The greater part of the time of the Congress, counted by hours, was given over to receptions and teas, breakfasts and dinners, visits to vineyards, public works and exhibitions, military tournaments, picnics and balls." Of the scientific meetings themselves he remembered little except that there were a lot of long speeches.

In truth, Bingham was bored. All of this reminded him too much of the stifling formality of the academic world and the family duties from which he had fled. He longed to get away from the fancy dinners and soft beds, and back to llama stew, filthy postes, and the freedom that they allowed.

As soon as the congress was over, Bingham was off on his travels once again, this time accompanied by a few delegates from the congress. The group paid a visit to the Peruvian port city of Mollendo, which Bingham had been assured was "one of those places where nature never intended man to live" and was "the worst harbor on the east coast of South America." He had expected "a surf-lashed landing place," where even in calm weather boats were "tossed about like a cockle shell, now thrown up towards heaven on the crest of a wave, now dropped down towards the nadir in its hollow." He was very much disappointed to find a rather ordinary and calm sort of harbor.

Mollendo also had the reputation of being the center for all manner of gruesome and infectious diseases, and Bingham had not intended to stay the night. But he missed the train and was forced to put up at the local hotel. The walls of the room were very thin, and in the next room was an English-speaking guest who was talking on the telephone to someone "who tried to frighten him out of his senses by vivid details as to the number of cases of 'yellow fever, bubonic plague and small pox' now raging in the town. 'More deaths occurring every day than the undertakers could possibly attend to!' 'Scarcely a house without its sick folk!!' 'Not a family still intact!!!' " Bingham decided not to try to check the accuracy of such rumors; he departed on the next available train.

He took a steamer across Lake Titicaca, the highest large body of water in the world, and ran into a terrific storm. He had unpleasant visions of "swimming in the water of a lake which is so cold that none of the Indians who live on its banks and navigate their crazy *balsas* over its surface have ever learned how to swim." The tiny, ancient steamer in which Bingham had crossed the lake somehow survived the storm, and Bingham got a full taste of "being tossed about like a cockle shell."

From Lake Titicaca he took a train to La Paz, capital of Bolivia. La Paz was a city dominated by the fierce Aymaras, which gave it in Bingham's words an "atmosphere of barbaric glitter which is lacking elsewhere."

Bingham wandered through teeming markets that sold everything from local pottery to dolls made in Germany. He was particularly fascinated by the huge variety of gambling games that seemed to be played everywhere. How his father and grandfather would have disapproved of his interest! In one of these games a little mechanical monkey was made to climb a pole and grab the winning number. Bingham bought a ticket and won, but it was decided that there had been something wrong in the way the game was played, and the numbers were rearranged. "The spring again set, and my luck changed, much to the delight of the Aymaras."

Along with the usual tourist attractions Bingham also visited the city jail, for he had heard it had a reputation for exceptional cruelty. The reputation he found was well deserved. "For our satisfaction the jailer unlocked the door of one cell, six feet high, three feet wide and eighteen inches deep. As the door opened, the occupant of the cell tumbled out onto the floor." It was, said Bingham, a "torture chamber." But the Bolivian official who had reluctantly given Bingham and his companions permission to visit the prison assured him that "it would be improved before long."

The next major stop on Bingham's journey was to be Cuzco, the old Inca capital. Getting there required a ride on the Bolivia railway. He had been told that this railway was so poorly constructed that there was at least one accident on every trip. Since Bingham had been traveling around South America he had learned to ignore such rumors, but this one happened to be correct. Just as Bingham began "to forget the delightful sense of approaching danger," the train in which he was riding quite literally fell off the tracks. No one was hurt and the damage was repaired in about an hour. Then it happened again. This time the accident was more serious and repairs took several hours. Bingham rode on, thinking evil thoughts about those who had built this miserable stretch of railroad.

The ride took Bingham past the ancient and mysterious ruins of Tiahuanaco. Bingham interrupted his journey long enough to take a closer look. Tiahuanaco is a ceremonial center built by a still unknown ancient people, who must once have controlled or at least influenced much of the Andean region. By the time the conquistadores arrived, the lords of Tiahuanaco had disappeared, and people had forgotten who had built the center. It was as mysterious to the Incas as it was to the Spanish. Amid what appear to be the remains of temples and palaces there was a great truncated pyramid. Bingham found that the pyramid had huge holes dug through it by treasure seekers looking for the "lost gold of the Incas." They never found any at Tiahuanaco.

Tiahuanaco had impressed and amazed many travelers, but not Hiram Bingham. The ruined monuments were nowhere near as large as he had expected. But he did admit that they had suffered greatly at the hands of the Spanish, who had hauled off stone to build churches in La Paz, and more recently at the hands of the railroad builders who had taken away five hundred trainloads of stone for building bridges and warehouses. Bingham felt no particular outrage at this destruction of ancient monuments. The young scholar's cavalier attitude toward antiquity was to change quickly and dramatically, for he had reached the town of Puno. Here Bingham happily bid good-bye to the last few delegates who had been traveling with him, and he prepared to take the train to Cuzco, the ancient capital of the Inca Empire, and to his destiny.

CHAPTER 5

Cuzco

Hiram Bingham had come to South America because he was bored with the life of a history teacher. His Bingham blood called for something more than the library and the lecture hall. He was ready to lead the "strenuous life" that Theodore Roosevelt had called for. Bingham's 1906 explorations had whetted his appetite for adventure and proved that he was physically tough enough for the role of explorer. His position as a delegate to the First Pan-American Congress at Santiago, Chile, in 1908, was little more than an excuse for an extended trip through the Andes and other parts of South America. But he wasn't yet the Hiram Bingham who was to be obsessed with finding the lost city of the Incas. Indeed, three-quarters of the way through his South American journey he showed little interest in the ancient history of South America.

Bingham had already traveled a considerable distance

over what had once been Inca roads. These he found more uncomfortable than interesting. The Bolivian highlands, part of the old Inca Empire, had merely depressed him. The Quechua Indians, descendants of the Incas and their subjects, struck him as an inoffensive and basically uninteresting folk, notable only for their extreme poverty, their addiction to chewing coca leaves, and their ability to run at high speeds through the thin mountain air.

The romance of an unknown past had not yet taken hold of the young American's tough and practical soul. The silent monoliths of the mysterious city of Tiahuanaco, which had sent generations of travelers into frenzies of wild speculation, left Bingham singularly unimpressed. The monoliths were smaller than he thought they were going to be and not very well made. Hiram Bingham was still more interested in modern politics than in lost cities.

Now Bingham was about to take the train to Cuzco, famed capital of the Inca Empire. To him it was just another city, and not one that had as much to recommend it as Sucre, Potosí, and La Paz. Indeed, most of what he had heard of Cuzco was bad, so he wasn't really looking forward to the trip. However, no well-traveled gentleman could visit Peru without visiting Cuzco.

The journey started inauspiciously, for Bingham arrived late at the railroad station at Puno and found that the train for Cuzco had already departed, one of the few times a South American train ever left on time, Bingham complained. The next train was not scheduled to arrive for several more days.

Normally Bingham wouldn't have minded the wait, but he was due to meet his old Yale buddy Clarence Hay on the Cuzco train, and Hay was to accompany him for the rest of the journey. This plan had now been seriously disrupted. But the prestige of being a *delegado* appeared to work miracles with the railway officials. When they found Bingham fuming and stomping angrily around the station, they promised to make up a special train just for him. This turned out to be only half a miracle, for when the train arrived it consisted of six freight cars and one tiny passenger coach. The coach was already occupied by Indian passengers who had crammed it so full of bags, bundles, and boxes that Bingham couldn't even squeeze in the door. So he eased his six-foot four-inch frame into the fireman's seat in the locomotive and stared out at the depressing scenery as the train rattled uncertainly up the mountains to La Oroya, 14,150 feet above sea level, and then shot abruptly, and alarmingly, downward to Sicuani. The trip had taken over eight hours, much longer than the schedule said it should. Bingham was cold, exhausted, and ferociously hungry. He joined the train crew as they stumbled through the pitch-dark streets of Sicuani in search of a meal. All they could find was a vile little *chichaería* run by a drunken proprietor and his equally drunken wife. At first they were told there was no food; however, by a combination of threats, pleas, and gross overpayment, Bingham and the crew got dinner. It was only tea, beer, and stale bread, but it was better than nothing. Bingham complained about the trip, but he was actually enjoying himself. This, he thought, was "real life."

Over beer the conductor told Bingham that the journey could not continue in the dark—it was far too dangerous and the little train would probably fall into the Vilcanota River, and everybody would be killed. When they got back to the station the conductor found a telegraph message waiting for him—the train must proceed the twenty-five miles to Checcacuppi that night so that the distinguished *delegado* would be able to catch the morning train that would take him to Cuzco.

Grumbling and muttering prayers, the conductor went back to his locomotive. Bingham looked into the tiny passenger car and found it was deserted—perhaps the Indians feared the night run to Checcacuppi. By now Bingham was just too exhausted to worry about what might happen. He rolled out his sleeping bag on the floor of the car, and the next thing he knew the station agent at Checcacuppi was shining a light in his face and telling him that he would not be disturbed until morning. He had slept through the entire dangerous trip. During the rest of the night Bingham was disturbed by sounds—scratchings and rumblings, as though some wild animal had gotten into the little car. Without a light Bingham couldn't investigate, and he was too tired to really care. If the thing was dangerous, so be it.

In the morning Bingham was awakened by the shouts of the trainmen who were making up the train for Cuzco. As he opened his eyes he spied his night-time visitor—not an animal at all—but a Quechua boy about seven years old. The boy spoke no Spanish, and Bingham spoke no Quechua. The boy indicated by sign language that he wished to accompany the American on his travels. Bingham wasn't quite sure how to handle this situation, but he did share his breakfast with the boy, who like most Quechuas looked half-starved.

A little while later Clarence Hay arrived. Hay had been hanging around Checcacuppi checking on all the trains. He knew that Hiram had to be on one of them, because this was the only way up to Cuzco. Bingham was delighted to see his old friend, and the pair was soon installed on the much more comfortable Cuzco train.

Bingham was beginning to feel more cheerful about the prospect of seeing the Inca capital. "How long will it take to reach Cuzco?" he asked a group of his fellow travelers. He never should have asked. Oh, days and days, they said, because the train ran alongside a steep valley and there were always landslides coming down from the heights and blocking the tracks. The train might not make it at all if it was unlucky enough to be caught in one of the landslides. Many people had already been killed on this dangerous section of track. The passengers gave this gloomy report in tones of absolute sincerity and utter resignation. They sounded like people who were ready to die if that was what fate had in store for them. Bingham's spirits sank. They sank even further when the conductor came up and politely announced that there was a boy in the second-class carriage who insisted that he was the American's slave! Now Bingham really didn't know what to do, but fortunately the problem was solved for him, for the boy disappeared shortly before the train reached Cuzco. And the train arrived on time—there wasn't a single landslide.

Bingham's first view of Cuzco did little to spark his enthusiasm for the capital city of the Incas. The railroad station at Cuzco was a cluster of corrugated iron buildings just outside the main part of the city. As Bingham and Hay rode into town they found that it amply lived up to its reputation as the filthiest city in all the Americas. The rough-paved stone streets were covered with slime, and the sewers were simply open channels that ran along the sides of the streets. Fortunately it was the rainy season and an occasional downpour cleansed the channels. In the dry season the streets were unspeakable. Even Bingham, who had never been squeamish, and who had been hardened by months of travel under the most primitive conditions, was sickened by the stench that surrounded him in the streets of Cuzco.

The Hotel Comercio, where the two Americans were lodged, proved to be an agreeable surprise. The rooms were large and reasonably clean and the food was more than edible. Of course, there were no toilets, but one should not expect too much in a fifteenth-century city, Bingham observed.

Like any ordinary tourists (which they were), Hiram Bingham and Clarence Hay strolled around the old Inca capital. The streets were thronged with Quechuas, the women in their brightly colored shawls, the men in brightly colored ponchos, and both wearing the distinctive pancake hats that were both decorative and good for keeping the rain off one's head. Would they have dressed so colorfully in the days of the Incas? The practical Bingham doubted it, for in every marketplace in the Andes, including those at Cuzco, Bingham had seen peddlers selling dyes imported from Europe—this was where the brilliant colors had come from, and all the hats were adorned with tinsel.

The city of Cuzco had been greatly changed since it had served as the Inca capital. Actually, no one really knows what the city looked like before the Spanish arrived. Only five Spanish saw the city before it was stripped of its gold to make up the ransom of Atahualpa, and not one of them left any written description. Even accounts of the city's appearance before much of it was destroyed during Manco Inca's great revolt are sketchy and unsatisfying. The conquistadores' civil wars added immeasurably to the destruction of the Inca capital, and the most damage of all was done by the Spanish builders who pulled down Inca structures and used the stone to build Spanish-style churches and houses. The conquistadores leveled the palaces of the Incas in order to construct their own palaces.

The Great Plaza of Cuzco had once been the ceremonial center of the entire Inca empire, the scene of some of the great Inca festivals that had so impressed the first Spanish in the region. The Great Plaza had also been the scene of appalling savagery. As Bingham wandered about the plaza, he recalled what he had read of the fate of an eighteenth-century Indian rebel leader who had taken the name Tupac Amaru, the last Inca. The Spanish had decided to make an example of him so that no other Indian would dare raise his hand against the conquerors—ever.

On the morning of May 18, 1781, Tupac Amaru and his principal *coya*, or wife, were led from the Jesuit church to the center of the plaza that was filled with silent Indians. The *coya* was placed on a high scaffold; then her tongue was cut out. The executioner made an attempt to garrote her with an iron screw, but her neck was too delicate, and she could not be strangled in that traditional manner. So the Spanish put a cord around her neck and dragged her around the plaza until she was dead.

Tupac Amaru was forced to witness this horrifying spectacle before it was his turn. He too was taken to the center of the plaza where his tongue was cut out. Then his body was cut open, and while he was still alive he was torn apart by four horses pulling in opposite directions.

The Spanish had been trying to stamp out the memory of the Incas for over 200 years. After the eighteenth-century rebellion by Tupac Amaru, the Spanish tried to prohibit the use of the Quechua language and all native customs and music. Had they succeeded? In a sense they had: the Spanish were never thrown out of Peru, and

Spanish remains the country's official language. But the victory had been far from complete.

As Bingham looked around the plaza he saw churches and Spanish-style buildings, but as he looked closer he realized that most of these buildings, indeed, most of the buildings in Cuzco, had been built on Inca foundations. The whitewash and the adobe applied by the Spanish in places had been chipped away, and the unpainted Inca stonework showed through. Many of the Spanish buildings had fallen during one or another of the earthquakes that regularly shake Cuzco. But what the Incas built had been able to withstand the quakes.

As he walked through the streets of Cuzco, Bingham found that nine out of ten of its inhabitants spoke and understood only Quechua, the language of the Incas, not Spanish, the language of the conquistadores, though the Spaniards had been in control of Cuzco for over five hundred years. Bingham discovered that basically Cuzco was still an Inca city. The Spanish had provided only a veneer. And for the first time the American traveler began to feel the lure of the Incas, whose buildings and culture had such a power to endure.

Bingham and Hay visited the warehouse of Don Cesar Lomellini, an Italian merchant who was reputed to be one of the richest men in Cuzco. Sr. Lomellini had developed a passion for the Incas and devoted all of his free time and a lot of his money to the study of Inca civilization. Even his warehouse was a monument to the Incas, for a fine old Inca doorway formed the entrance. Sr. Lomellini himself had his home built on what was supposed to be the site of the palace of Manco Capac, the legendary founder of the Inca Empire. Sr. Lomellini talked enthusiastically of the remarkable skills of the former lords of Cuzco, and he showed Bingham some finely carved bronze figures that looked as though they had been buried for centuries in the tombs of the Incas.

"Beautiful," said Bingham.

"Fake," said Sr. Lomellini. "Made in Germany," he added with a sad smile. "Almost everything the tourists buy today has been made in Germany or somewhere else. So little of what the Incas made remains. It was all taken away and melted down centuries ago. What a waste. What a crime. The greatness of the Incas can now only be seen in the stones. But what stones!"

Sr. Lomellini told the Americans that they must go to Sacsahuaman, the great fortress above the city. There they would see the finest stones in the world. And when they returned from the fortress they could visit his home and talk more of the glories of the ancient Incas.

Bingham and Hay already had planned a visit to Sacsahuaman; everyone who came to Cuzco had to visit Sacsahuaman.

This citadel was to be the ultimate, unassailable haven for the Lord Inca and his army in case Cuzco was ever overwhelmed by an attack. Exactly when the fortress was built is unknown. Also unknown is whether the Incas ever successfully used it for defense. It was certainly of no use against Pizarro, who simply rode into an unresisting Cuzco and took it over in 1533. During the great rebellion of 1536, Manco had been able to capture Sacsahuaman, but the Spanish were able to take it back again. While the fortress would probably have been able to withstand the attack of any Indian army, it would not have been able to withstand European cannons and siege techniques. Successful or not, Sacsahuaman is an incredible feat of construction.

The fortress is built on a hill about a mile outside of Cuzco, not much of a walk on level ground, but Cuzco's elevation is 11,500 feet above sea level, and Sacsahuaman is 600 feet above that. Bingham and Hay hired mules for the trip. The city street they traveled along became a path through a rocky gorge. At the narrowest part of the gorge the two men were suddenly confronted with a gateway over twelve feet high, made of huge blocks of roughly hewn stone. Beyond this gate was a path along which ran a wall of boulders. This was the main entrance to the fortress. An invading army would have to squeeze its way single file through this passage, and they could be attacked from above with stones and other missiles.

From the top of the hill the other defenses of Sacsahuaman could be seen. The side of the hill facing the city is extremely steep, and its approach was made even more difficult by a series of three terraces, each twelve feet high. That was not the direction from which the Incas expected an attack. It was the other side of the hill, the side facing away from the city, where the Incas constructed their most elaborate fortifications and the builders showed their true genius. Here the slope is gentle, an obvious attraction to an invading army. The Incas fortified this side of the hill with three zigzag walls, made up of enormous boulders—some of them twelve to fourteen feet across. The lower wall averaged twenty-five feet in height and had probably once been higher, but the smaller stones were carted away after the Spanish conquest, to be used in other constructions. The two upper walls were about six feet in height.

Hiram Bingham was suddenly, and surprisingly, awed by the sight. Of course he had read the accounts of other travelers, and he has seen pictures of the walls of Sacsahuaman, but none of this prepared him for the overpowering sight of the walls themselves. Pictures showed only a small portion of the walls and gave no true impression of their extent. Words were totally inadequate. These walls were the most impressive spectacle of human achievement that Bingham had seen in his travels. As Bingham gazed at these colossal and utterly unique structures, he began to succumb to the lure and mystery of the ancient and vanished civilization of the Incas. His conversion from superior and skeptical teacher to dedicated explorer had begun.

What impressed Bingham most was not the sheer size of the walls, but the way in which they were constructed. The individual blocks of stone were huge; he estimated the weight of the biggest stones to be as much as 200 tons. The blocks were irregularly cut, each one having its own particular shape, yet they had been fitted together so carefully that not even the blade of a knife could be inserted between them. Without the use of mortar or cement, these walls had stood for centuries in an area regularly racked by earthquakes. The early conquistadores had been amazed by the walls of Sacsahuaman. So was Hiram Bingham.

The wheel was unknown to the Incas, not that it would have done them much good in their vertical empire. They had no beasts of burden more powerful than the llama, which is not very strong. They didn't have pulleys or the use of squares and levels to determine the fit of the stones. How could they possibly have built anything on the scale of this fortress?

That is a question that practically everyone who has ever viewed these colossal walls has asked. The answers they have given have ranged from the practical to the fanciful. One theory that Bingham had heard was that the Incas knew of some plant, the juice of which could temporarily render stones soft so that they could be fitted together perfectly.

Bingham wasn't much attracted to fanciful theories. To him there was nothing mysterious about the methods of construction. It was done with the simplest of tools: ropes, rollers, and inclined planes. The secret, if it could be called that, was the patient and well-organized labor of thousands and thousands of Indians over a long period of time. In his account of his visit he wrote, "Nevertheless, when one considers the difficulties of fitting together two irregular boulders . . . one's admiration for the skill of these old builders knows no bounds."

On the way down from the fortress Bingham and Hay visited the home of Sr. Lomellini, the home that Italian merchant had built on the site of the palace of the first Manco, founder of the Inca Empire. Like the palaces of the other Incas, this one had stood in the shadow of the walls of Sacsahuaman. The enthusiastic merchant showed the Americans some of the Inca treasures he had obtained. There wasn't much gold, he admitted, but "out there"—he waved his hang vaguely in a northerly direction—there was so much hidden, so much left to be discovered. The land of the Incas, he said, was still a land of mystery.

Bingham received this second lecture on the wonders of the vanished Inca civilization with more interest than he had the first. Though he didn't know it at the time, the course of his life had been changed.

As Bingham and Hay mounted their mules for the ride down to Cuzco, Sr. Lomellini's gardener presented them with roses. The mules made their way over the rough cobblestones of Cuzco, and Bingham could still joke about the "picturesque sights—and distressing smells" of the city. But modern Cuzco was merely a shadow of what it had once been. The real glory of Cuzco lay in its Inca past. Bingham had arrived in Cuzco on a train—that made him little more than a tourist. If he was to be a true adventurer, he had to leave the city as the Incas had left it, on their royal highway. Sane travelers avoided the Inca highway in 1908. It was a trip that was difficult at best and had a reputation for being dangerous. Bingham didn't care—that was what he wanted now. The trip would be a chance to test himself once again and perhaps to find something that no one had ever found before. He wasn't sure what, yet. Maybe it would be the solution to one of those mysteries of the Incas of which Sr. Lomellini had spoken.

CHAPTER 6

"The Cradle of Gold"

Lima, the capital of modern Peru, was to be the final
stop on Bingham's grand tour of South America. There
were several ways to go from Cuzco to Lima. Bingham
chose to travel the most difficult route but also the most
historic. Most of the three hundred miles of the trip was
to be made along the old Inca highway from Cuzco to
Huancayo.

The road had been there even before the Incas. The
Incas had taken it, improved it, and used it as the principal highway for their conquests to the north. The largest
part of Atahualpa's golden ransom was carried from
Cuzco over this road. When Pizarro and his little band
marched to the Inca capital to complete their easy
takeover, they had used the road. The road figured
prominently in Manco's great revolt and in the civil wars
with which the conquistadores consumed themselves.
The road was also used by Peruvian rebels who cast off
the colonial rule of Spain in 1824. In short, the road from
Cuzco to Huancayo had seen a lot of history. However,
by 1909 road travel had been replaced by rail travel, and

the historic highway was rarely used anymore and had fallen into disrepair.

Before departing, Bingham had been treated to all the usual gloomy warnings about the dangers and hardships of the trip he was about to undertake. He was told that the road was impassable, that the land was uninhabited, and that the travelers would find no food for themselves and no fodder for their mules. Bingham was getting used to hearing this sort of talk, and he had learned to ignore the doomsayers.

What he could not ignore was the rain. Bingham and Hay scheduled their departure for February 1. February is the height of the rainy season in the Peruvian highlands, and this was to be the rainiest month of the rainiest season that anyone could remember. Bingham wasn't sorry, he was exhilarated. Other travelers had described the journey during the dry season, but "we were to see the mountain trails at their worst!"

On the morning of their departure the rain was so bad that the usual delegation of local dignitaries didn't even show up to usher the Americans out of town. Everywhere else Bingham had been, his departure was marked by a sort of ceremonial procession of local notables. It seemed to be a South American custom. But then the weather had been better. The local prefect, however, had insisted that the two Americans had to be accompanied on their entire trip by a military escort, which was to be paid for by the government. Bingham didn't need an escort and didn't want one; however, he could find no convenient way of turning down the favor, so two wet and unhappy Peruvian soldiers trudged along with them.

All the dire rumors proved to be false. Far from being uninhabited, the land along the road was dotted with villages in which the travelers were warmly welcomed. Nor was the region anywhere near as remote as Bingham had been led to believe. In one of the villages he found an upright piano in remarkably good tune. He was told that that piano had been carried along the road from Cuzco on the backs of Indian bearers. Before the rail line had been built, the Indians had carted objects as heavy as pianos up the mountains to Cuzco from the coast. These were the very descendants of the people who had dragged the boulders to the walls of Sacsahuaman. No wonder Bingham put no stock in tales of magical plant juice. He had seen what human labor could accomplish in the mountains of Peru.

Evidence of the vanished Inca Empire was everywhere along the road. It was in the crumbling stone roadway beneath the hooves of their mules. It could be seen in vegetation-covered but still recognizable terraces, walls, and stairways built into the mountains above the road. The farther Bingham traveled now, the more impressed he became with the power and ingenuity of the Incas. Neither the Spanish nor the jungle could obliterate them.

The dignitaries of the villages had all been cordial to the Americans, but at the town of Abancay their reception was overwhelming. Word of the coming of the Americans had been sent on ahead, and all the local officials and leading planters rode out to greet them. Bingham and Hay were given the best rooms at the town's club (there was no hotel) and were told that a grand reception and banquet in their honor had been planned for that very evening.

Bingham suspected that something more than simple hospitality was operating here, and it wasn't long before his suspicions were confirmed. The prefect asked Bingham and Hay if they had ever heard of Choqquequirau. In the Quechua language the word means "the cradle of gold."

Choqquequirau was a spot not far from Abancay where Inca ruins were located. According to tradition the place had once been a major Inca city with at least fifteen thousand inhabitants. It was a place where the Incas were said to have hidden some of the gold destined for Atahualpa's ransom, lest it fall into the hands of his murderers. According to another tradition, Choqquequirau was Vilcapampa, the last refuge of the last Incas, and it still contained the treasure that they had managed to save. Somehow all of these stories revolved around the magic word *gold*.

Choqquequirau was the most interesting place one could imagine, the prefect told Bingham, and he really should take the time to pay it a visit. Bingham was puzzled. He had never heard of Choqquequirau. None of the many travel volumes he had read to prepare for his journey had mentioned it.

The request to visit "the cradle of gold" was pressed at the reception and banquet that evening. This event was attended by everyone of importance and influence in the vicinity of Abancay. As the details of the proposed trip emerged, Bingham saw that he was not being asked to take an easy half-day excursion.

True enough, the ruins were not far from Abancay, but much of the distance was straight up, and in order to get there, one had to cross over one of the world's wildest rivers on a tiny swinging bridge. Choqquequirau was perched atop a ridge some six thousand feet above the madly rushing waters of the Apurímac River. In modern times only a few bold mountain climbers had ever managed to reach the ruins, and they returned half dead and filled with garbled tales that only seemed to deepen the mystery of "the cradle of gold" and inspire further exploration.

The lure of gold had so excited the notables of Abancay that they had banded together to form a treasure-hunting company. After spending a great deal of time and money, the company had been able to construct a trail of sorts from Abancay to the ruins. When Bingham asked about the nature of the trail, the notables quickly turned the conversation to another subject. But one man told him candidly that he had tried the trail and would never attempt the trip again because he had very nearly been killed falling from a precipice. It wasn't going to be an easy trip.

The prefect and others told Bingham that they wanted the "Yanqui scientist" and his "secretary" (that was Hay) to examine the ruins before any more treasure-hunting activities were carried out. Finally he was told that President Leguía of Peru himself had asked the treasure hunters to suspend operations until the ruins could be viewed by the "scientist."

Bingham protested that he wasn't a scientist, he was merely a delegate to a scientific convention, and that his appointment had been political not scientific. He knew nothing about the Incas and he had not come to South America to look for Inca ruins.

The banquet stretched on late into the evening. Toast after toast was drunk. There were more tales of the golden wonders of the Incas, and more flattery for the distinguished American "scientist." Everybody was absolutely sure the American was just being modest about his many accomplishments. Bingham, who towered over everyone else in the room, was constantly having his sleeve pulled or his shoulder tapped by some official who told him how wonderful he was, and what a great honor it would be to have him visit Choqquequirau.

Finally after a long evening and many, many toasts Bingham was able to recall what Elihu Root, U.S. secretary of state, had told him when he was appointed delegate to the scientific congress in the first place: "Be sure and cooperate with all of the local officials you meet during your travels so as to generate international goodwill." Here, thought Bingham, was an opportunity to generate a lot of goodwill.

With a show of great reluctance, Hiram Bingham gave in to the entreaties of his hosts. Yes, he and Clarence Hay would start for Choqquequirau as soon as they recovered from the banquet. There were cheers, smiles, and more toasts drunk all round. Bingham fell into bed that night not quite sure what he had gotten himself and his friend into.

All of Bingham's protests had been nonsense, of course. The moment he heard of lost cities of gold, he decided that he was going to make the trip. He had merely been looking for a plausible excuse to interrupt his journey to go wandering off after this romantic vision. The next morning when he awoke, Bingham found his room filling up with blankets, saddles, and packages of food, presents for the trip from the local notables.

A day later when Bingham and Hay felt somewhat better, the trip began. For the first few miles Bingham had the uncomfortable feeling that practically everyone in Abancay was going to accompany them, leaving the town deserted. The usual procession at leave-taking had been turned into a grand parade. But it was raining hard, and the trail was in terrible shape. The crowd quickly melted away. The final expedition consisted of Bingham and Hay, a few soldiers, an irrepressibly enthusiastic guide named Caceres, and two young men from Abancay who were having their first real adventure. Then there was the line of silent, patient Quechua porters.

The journey continued throughout the day, on a trail that grew steadily worse. By about five in the afternoon Bingham began to hear a tremendous roaring sound that grew louder, the farther they went. It was the Apurímac River. At this point the river was about 250 feet wide but nearly 100 feet deep. An enormous volume of water was being forced through a narrow gorge, and the resulting roar could be heard for miles. In Quechua, *Apurímac* means "great speaker."

The trail was blocked by a fallen tree and partially ripped away by an avalanche, and by the time these difficulties had been surmounted, it was quite dark. In the Andes where the setting sun is blocked by the mountains, darkness falls quickly. The little group still had to descend six thousand feet to a camp that had been set up by the river's edge. Caceres told them the rest of the trip was all "level ground." It was his little joke.

In retrospect, Bingham was glad that he had negotiated the descent in the dark, otherwise he might have turned back. The trail corkscrewed down the wall of the canyon in short turns of about twenty feet. At each end of the turn there was a sheer drop. The trail itself was less than two feet wide.

Bingham could hear their irrepressible Caceres shouting words of encouragement over the roar of the river. In total darkness there was nothing that Bingham could do but trust to the abilities of his sure-footed mule. But about halfway down, the mule suddenly stopped short and started trembling. When Bingham dismounted, he found that the mule had wandered off the trail onto a ledge. Somehow Bingham managed to back the animal up and onto the trail again, but he had lost confidence in it. He walked the rest of the way down holding the mule by the tail. If the mule was going to fall over the edge, it was going to go alone.

The camp by the river's edge consisted of nothing more than a few reed huts, but simply to arrive at the end of that trail in one piece was its own reward. One of the young men from Abancay had become so unstrung by the dangerous descent that he began wildly firing his pistol during the night; at least that is what the guide told Bingham the next morning. As usual, Bingham had been able to sleep through the excitement.

In the morning the travelers faced the next obstacle in their journey, the rushing waters of the Apurímac itself. The river was spanned by a frail-looking suspension bridge 275 feet long and 33 inches wide. Bingham and Hay were introduced to the bridge's remarkable builder, an aged Chinese peddler who had been wandering the mountains of Peru for over thirty years and had picked up the Spanish name of Don Mariano.

When the treasure-hunting company decided to construct a trail to Choqquequirau, they knew they would have to build a bridge over the rapids of the Apurímac. No one could be found to undertake the task, until finally Don Mariano volunteered. He picked a time when the river was only twenty-five feet deep and relatively calm. He then swam it with a string tied around his waist. After a great deal of effort Don Mariano had managed to secure six strands of telegraph wire across the Apurímac. From these he hung short lengths of rope. To serve as a footpath he wove a mat of reeds about two feet wide. Since the bridge had been built, the river had risen fifty feet, and it now boiled up less than thirty feet from the footpath, which swayed crazily in the wind. That was what Bingham and his party now had to cross. (The bridge was later swept away by the river, but the original strands of telephone wire could still be seen spanning the river in the 1960s.)

There was no possibility that the pack animals could ever be induced to cross that bridge. Besides they would have been useless in making the final ascent on the other side. Even the Indian porters were terrified, and they hesitantly crept across the suspension bridge on their hands and knees. For centuries their ancestors had confidently crossed frail, swaying suspension bridges built by the Incas. But these bridges had been constructed with thick rope—it was the thin wire that the Indians distrusted. Though in reality the wire was much stronger than the thick rope, the Indians didn't have any confidence in such flimsy-looking support. Bingham and Hay also made the crossing on their hands and knees.

Once the river was crossed it was only a short distance to the ruins of "the cradle of gold"; unfortunately that distance was straight up. Bingham had been up a lot of mountains since he came to South America, but most of his climbing had been done on the back of a mule or horse, with the animal doing all the work. Now he was on his own, and it was hard. Neither he nor Hay was an experienced mountaineer, so they scrambled and crawled their way up the side of the mountain, stopping to rest and gasp for breath about every fifty feet. They crossed streams on slippery logs or treacherous little stone foot bridges. Up ahead their guide and cheerleader, Caceres, kept shouting "Onward!" and "Valor!" to encourage them. The Americans didn't feel very valorous, and the only satisfaction they got was that they were able to outclimb the young men from Abancay.

As they neared the top, the climbers began to see

evidence of Inca habitation—the remains of terraces, the most characteristic of all Inca structures. So it was true; in this wildly impossible, very nearly inaccessible spot the Incas had indeed constructed a city.

As the two Americans scrambled to an open spot in order to get a better view of their surroundings, they found that they themselves were under observation by a gigantic condor, the largest of all flying birds. Bingham estimated that the bird had a wingspan of about twelve feet. We now know that condors are not normally aggressive, but Bingham had heard all sorts of stories about how condors carried off sheep and children and attacked climbers. At that moment he believed every one of the tales because he had never seen such a large, mean-looking bird. He wasn't at all sure of the creature's peaceful intentions. The condor swooped close enough so that the Americans could see its great talons, its curved beak, even the whites of its eyes. Bingham was unarmed and he looked around for a stick, a rock, or anything with which to fend off the giant bird's expected attack. Then suddenly, apparently without changing the position of a single feather, the condor soared away, leaving the Americans very much relieved.

After spending an extremely uncomfortable night, Bingham and Hay set out to explore the Inca city. The treasure-hunting company had done a good job in clearing the jungle from the ruins. It was immediately obvious that Choqquequirau was not the great city of gold that the enthusiastic treasure hunters from Abancay had hoped it was. However, it was unquestionably an Inca ruin of considerable size. The buildings were constructed of rough stone laid in clay. The stonework was nowhere near as fine as the Inca stonework of Cuzco, but it was very similar to the construction used in buildings in other parts of the Inca domains. Bingham had the impression that Choqquequirau had been one of a line of fortress outposts built to protect the heart of the Inca empire from the attack of unconquered tribes from the great forest below. Bingham thought that a bonfire lighted on the heights of Choqquequirau could have been one of a series of signal fires used to flash a message to Cuzco.

All of this Bingham freely admitted was nothing more than sheer guesswork. Bingham and Hay spent four days at Choqquequirau, much of the time stumbling about the ruins, not being quite sure what they were supposed to do. Bingham had been hailed as "a scientist" and an "expert," but in truth he was the rankest of amateurs. All he knew about archaeology was contained in a book he carried called *Hints to Travelers*, published by the Royal Geographical Society in England. The book suggested that when a traveler is confronted by an archaeological site he was supposed to do three things. First, take plenty of photographs; second, make careful measurements; and third, describe all the finds as accurately as possible.

Unfortunately the weather was awful—the humidity was always near 100 percent, and when it wasn't actually raining, the area was wrapped in clouds or mist. The result was that most of the photos Bingham took didn't come out. "It was not a pleasant introduction to archaeological reconnaissance," he recalled.

Still, with his characteristic enthusiasm and determination Bingham proceeded to measure and observe everything that he could and to make lengthy notes in his notebook. The buildings he found were clustered in three distinct groups, and all were crammed as closely together as possible so as to make use of every inch of level ground.

There was a sheer precipice on every side of the site, and all the possible approaches had been elaborately fortified by the Incas. To Bingham it seemed as if Choqquequirau had been virtually inaccessible and impregnable to attack. It would also have been to a degree self-sustaining, for the terraces served a double purpose of defense and holding soil for gardens. There were the remains of a system for collecting rainwater. The ingenuity that the Incas displayed in building and maintaining their vertical empire was astonishing.

Of gold, however, there wasn't the smallest trace, and Bingham doubted if any would be found. He wondered why the place would have been called "the cradle of gold" at all. One theory he proposed was that from a distance the ridge on which Choqquequirau lies looks a bit like a hammock, and the setting sun might have given it a golden tinge. His other theory was that "the cradle of gold" was just a modern invention, since the name did not appear in any of the old records. It might have been the wish or fantasy of some unknown gold seekers.

In the rare moments when the mists cleared sufficiently for the travelers to get a clear view of their surroundings, they could catch glimpses of the mighty Apurímac River in the canyon six thousand feet below. From that height the great boiling torrent looked like a tiny silver brook. Cataracts of water, one with a clear fall of at least a thousand feet, crashed down from the heights into the valley. Bingham had never viewed scenery so magnificent.

He was really more impressed by the scenery than by

the ruins. He concluded that, far from being "the cradle of gold," Choqquequirau was an outpost, and not a very important one at that. The Incas had left behind very little in the way of artifacts when they abandoned Choqquequirau. The treasure hunters had found a few pots and a club of some sort. At first the club created a great deal of excitement, for it had a yellowish tinge and was thought to be made of gold. It turned out to be bronze. Bingham himself found a small spindle whorl bob of the type that was still used by Indian women all over the Andes for spinning wool. That was about all the ruins yielded.

Under the walls of the city, workmen had found caves that served as burial places for the inhabitants of Choqquequirau. Traditionally the Incas dried the bodies of their dead and made mummies of them. The mummies of the Lord Incas were the most venerated objects in the Inca Empire and were carried around on ceremonial occasions. Attempts were also made to preserve the bodies of more ordinary folk. In the dry coastal deserts of Peru, Inca mummies were well preserved, but here in the rain-soaked highlands they had not endured well. Bingham found that apparently solid-looking bones crumbled to damp powder when he tried to pick them up. Aside from the rotting bones themselves, the graves contained practically nothing. There were two possible reasons for this: either the graves had already been rifled, for the site had been visited a few times before the treasure hunters of Abancay reached it, or, and this Bingham thought more likely, Inca nobles who died at this frontier outpost were removed to some other place for burial, and only the poor were placed in the caves. The poor had nothing to leave behind.

The Indian bearers had watched with a complete lack of interest as the Americans climbed around taking pictures and making measurements and notes. When Bingham and Hay began to examine the bones, the Indians suddenly became interested. Now all of this apparently pointless activity made sense. The Americans had come all the way to Choqquequirau in order to communicate with the spirits of the dead Incas! And in a sense the Indians were right as far as Hiram Bingham was concerned. If he had not actually been communicating with the dead Incas, he was at least captivated by their spirit.

The prefect of Abancay and his treasure-hunting partners were deeply disappointed when Bingham returned and reported that he was unable to find any evidence of hidden treasure, and delivered the opinion that there probably was no gold to be found in "the cradle of gold." But Bingham himself was far from personally disappointed. Although he had just spent an exhausting week, facing dangers and extreme discomfort without finding a hint of the gold that had launched him on his quest in the first place, nevertheless, he was exhilarated. He had become one of the first people in modern times to visit a lost city. It may have been an unimportant outpost, but it had been an outpost of the greatest and most mysterious civilization of the Americas. Bingham was now convinced that other and grander cities were out there in the unexplored mountains of Peru just waiting to be discovered by anyone bold enough to make the attempt.

He described his feelings at that moment by quoting lines from British writer Rudyard Kipling's 1898 poem "The Explorer":

"Something hidden. Go and find it. Go and look behind the
    Ranges—
Something lost behind the Ranges. Lost and waiting for you.
    Go!"

CHAPTER 7

Off the Map

Hiram Bingham returned from South America fired with enthusiasm for exploration. He wanted to find the lost gold of the Incas. He wanted to find the lost cities of the Incas. He wanted to explore the little-known portions of the Andes. He wanted to do something great, something that would make the world take notice of him.

During the summer of 1910 Bingham was in New Haven. He had written a book about his South American adventures and was reading the proofs and dreaming of getting back there somehow. He was asked to review another book on South America, this one written by Professor Adolph Bandelier. In a footnote he found a reference to Nevado Coropuna (Mount Coropuna), which according to the professor was the highest mountain in South America.

"I knew the thrill of that great and hazardous sport [mountain climbing]. My sensations when I read Bandelier's footnote are difficult to describe. . . ." Bingham had never heard of Coropuna before. He couldn't find the mountain on any of the standard maps, but he finally did manage to locate it on detailed maps made by an explorer named Antonio Riamondi. It was located due south of Choqquequirau and the hidden lands "behind the ranges" that he had been told about. Somewhere back in that remote and unknown region may have been the location of Manco II's capital.

Sitting in the quiet and comfort of Connecticut that summer, Hiram Bingham began to dream. His dream was to lead an expedition across the wildest part of Peru, to look for the lost city, the gold, and anything else he might find, and then climb Coropuna in the bargain. Bingham had no specific idea as to how this particular dream was to be financed. There were limits, even to the Tiffany fortune.

In the winter Bingham went to a class dinner at the Yale Club in New York. Since his travels had gained him a certain amount of fame, he was asked to deliver a speech. "Naturally I spoke of what was on my mind." What was on his mind were his plans and dreams to penetrate the lands "behind the ranges." He spoke so enthusiastically and eloquently that afterward his class-mates rushed up to congratulate him. Some of the younger Yale men wanted to go along on the expedition as assistants; the older and wealthier ones offered to pay part of the expenses. Bingham was surprised, over-whelmed, and absolutely delighted.

And so in this rather haphazard fashion the Yale Pe-ruvian expedition was formed. The expedition consisted of Professor Isaiah Bowman, geologist-geographer; Pro-fessor Harry Foote, naturalist; Dr. William G. Erving, surgeon; Karl Hendrickson, topographer; H. L. Tucker, engineer; and Paul B. Lanius, assistant. Naturally Hiram Bingham III was head of the expedition. The little band left New York in June of 1911 and arrived in Lima, Peru, late in the month.

Bingham wasn't quite sure where to start looking. In Lima he was shown the chronicle written by Father Calanacha, who had collected reports from missionaries who had lived in the lands under the control of the great rebel Inca, Manco II. There had always been considerable confusion as to the name of Manco's capital. It had often been called Vilcapampa. But Father Calanacha wrote of a city called Vitcos. Was this another name for the capital or were there really two lost cities? Bingham didn't know, and the maps and other chronicles gave a thoroughly confusing picture. But Father Calanacha indicated that Vitcos lay in the valley of the Urubamba River, and since most previous searchers did not have the advantage of having seen this particular chronicle, Bingham believed that this would make a promising start for his expedition. He would try to find Calanacha's Vitcos.

Any expedition into the Inca heartland must really start from Cuzco, and there Bingham renewed his friendship with the Italian merchant and Inca enthusiast Don Cesar Lomellini. With Sr. Lomellini's assistance, the expedition managed to buy supplies, organize a mule train, hire guides and bearers, get the approval of the governmental authorities, and otherwise do all those things that were necessary for successfully launching an exploration of this remote and difficult region.

Bingham visited the university in Cuzco, where the professors told him there were no ruins of interest in the Urubamba Valley. Bingham was not in the least discouraged. He had visited the university on his previous trip and had not been impressed. He had described it as "squalid."

Bingham also made the rounds of the clubs and bars of Cuzco, introducing himself to planters and prospectors and anyone else who might have any knowledge of the Urubamba Valley and about some of the places mentioned by Father Calanacha. Most of the men he talked to had never heard of Vitcos or the other places mentioned in the Spanish priest's chronicle, but two or three did say that there were Inca ruins in the valley. "And one old prospector said there were interesting ruins at Machu Picchu." It was the first time Bingham heard that name, and it did not leave much of a mark on his consciousness at that moment. One thing that every South American explorer quickly learned was that there were always rumors of ruins or of some other wonderful find out there somewhere. Most of these rumors turned out to be wild exaggerations or complete falsehoods. So when Bingham and his party finally did set out into the Urubamba Valley, they were not looking specifically for Machu Picchu.

As the Yale expedition descended from the chilly heights of Cuzco into the valley, they first passed through a veritable wonderland. The gardens were full of roses and lilies and other brilliant flowers. There were orchards of peaches, pears, and apples, and fields of luscious strawberries. This area had been a favored resort for the Incas. But the scenery quickly grows wilder, and at the town of Torontoy the pleasant cultivated valley comes to an end, and one enters the Grand Canyon of the Urubamba. A road, of sorts, had been cut into the valley along the river in 1895.

"The river road ran recklessly up and down rock stairways, blasted its way beneath overhanging precipices, spanned chasms on frail bridges propped on rustic brackets against granite cliffs." All around them in this difficult land, with virtually no level ground, the members of the expedition found signs of the occupation of the Incas. Bingham was impressed. "Emotions came thick and fast. We marveled at the exquisite pains with which the ancient folk had rescued incredibly narrow strips of arable land from the tumbling rapids. How could they ever have managed to build a retaining wall along the very edge of a dangerous river, which it is death to cross?"

As the party proceeded down the river road, they could see more Inca ruins on the other side of the river, but there was no possible way to cross the raging Urubama.

They pushed onward until they reached a curiously named place called La Máquina, "the machine." When Bingham asked what the name meant, he was told that several large iron wheels, parts from a "machine" destined for a sugar plantation in the valley, had been dragged to this spot but could be taken no farther. They had been abandoned and left to rust in the jungle. Since there was no fodder for the mules at "the machine," the party was forced to push onward over a section of the road that had been blasted out of the face of a granite cliff. Part of the road had simply fallen into the river and had been repaired by a bridge of logs, branches, and reeds. It was a toss-up as to whether the mules or the men were more nervous making the crossing.

Dusk, which falls quickly in the deep canyons, had engulfed Bingham and his companions as they completed their traverse of the treacherous path, and entered a little open plain called Mandor Pampa, which was hemmed in on all sides by the mountains or the rushing river. On this small bit of level ground there stood a single, ill-kept grass hut. This was the residence of Mandor Pampa's sole inhabitant, Melchor Arteaga, a Quechua farmer who also fancied himself an innkeeper when the rare traveler happened by.

Arteaga was suspicious of these strangers who were

so blithely ignoring his "inn" and setting up camp nearby. But the party's escort Sergeant Carrasco, who spoke Quechua, had a long and reassuring conversation with Arteaga. When the innkeeper heard that the foreigners were looking for Inca ruins, he said that he knew of some very good ones "up there" and pointed vaguely to a mountaintop on the other side of the river. He also promised that he would guide the party to the ruins the very next day.

The events of that day, July 24, 1911, have already been described in Chapter 1. That is the dreamlike day on which Hiram Bingham first gazed upon the ruins of Machu Picchu. Over the next four days Bingham wandered about the unknown city that he had discovered, measuring, recording, and taking photographs where he could. It was a city of magnificent temples, palaces, and plazas connected by an astonishing network of streets and more stairways than he had ever seen anywhere in his life. All of this was built at a dizzying and almost inaccessible height. Most significantly, this city had not been destroyed but had simply been abandoned. It was the only completely intact Inca city ever found. Bingham knew that he had made an extremely important discovery, though the thick vegetation that obscured his view of many of the buildings kept him from realizing just how remarkable a find it was. Besides, there was much more to be discovered, and as usual Hiram Bingham was in a hurry. So he climbed down from the heights of Machu Picchu to see what else he could find.

Whatever Machu Picchu was, and at this point Bingham had no idea, it was not the Vitcos mentioned in Calanacha's chronicle. No real description of the city was given by Father Calanacha, but it was clearly not in the mountains. Calanacha had written, "Close by Vitcos in a village called Chuquipalta is a House of the Sun and in it a white stone over a spring of water." Such a description could not apply to the mountaintop city at Machu Picchu. So Bingham pushed onward down the Urubamba Valley. He offered cash rewards for anyone who could bring him news of Inca ruins and a double bonus for ruins that fit the description of the Temple of the Sun, which was supposed to be near Vitcos.

The planters of the valley were intrigued by Bingham's offer, and they sent their workers out in all directions to look for ruins. Inevitably, stories of ruins came back by the dozen. Experience had already taught Bingham to be skeptical of many of the stories that he heard. Yet it was on the basis of just such a vague rumor that he had found the ruins at Machu Picchu, so he felt bound to check out as many of the tales as he could.

One story seemed particularly intriguing, for it came from a place known locally as Yurac-rumi, or "white stone." Here, according to an apparently trustworthy informant, were the remains of an Inca city. Since Bingham knew that Vitcos lay near a place with a large white stone, he became quite excited. "Here was a definite statement made by an eyewitness. Apparently we were about to see that interesting rock where the last Incas worshipped."

There were difficulties. The ruins lay in a part of the jungle so dense that it took a week just to clear a path to the place. When the path was finally cleared, Bingham started with great high hopes. He expected that the size of the ruins had been exaggerated. "Still it never entered my head what I was actually to find." After many more hours spent clearing the jungle from the walls, Bingham found that the "extensive ruins" consisted of a single house, and a rather primitive one at that. After the exhilaration of the great find at Machu Picchu, the disappointment of Yurac-rumi was keen.

So Bingham pushed on into the jungle of the valley of the Vilcabamba River, which joins the Urubamba. Here the noise of the roaring river was so loud in the narrow valley that it made normal conversation impossible. And this was the dry season! Bingham wondered what the river would sound like in the rainy season.

There were more ruins, some marked on maps, some previously unknown. But none was very impressive or fit the description of Vitcos. And as always, there was a profusion of strange and confusing names. He found ruins at a place called Incahuaracana, which translated means "the place where the Inca shoots with a sling." Which Inca? Bingham wondered.

After numerous false starts and disappointments Bingham finally followed his guides to the top of a hill called Rosaspata, Hill of the Roses. Here he found the ruins of an Inca fortress. They were in a ruinous condition indeed. Unlike those at Machu Picchu, which had remained virtually untouched from the time the city was abandoned, these ruins had repeatedly been plundered by treasure hunters and by farmers looking for cut stones with which to build their own houses. Yet enough remained at Rosaspata to indicate to Bingham that this had once been a formidable fortress. "The side of easiest approach is protected by a splendid long wall, built so carefully as not to leave a single toe-hold for active besiegers." It was the sort of place where the last Incas could have hoped to hold off the Spanish.

Was this Vitcos? Bingham searched his notes for all the references he could find. They were scattered, incomplete, and all too often contradictory. It was a jigsaw puzzle with most of the pieces missing. But Bingham thought that this shattered fortress in which he stood could have been Manco's Vitcos, the place where he was so unaccountably murdered by the Spanish renigades. However, there was not enough left of the site to be certain of the identification. He still needed to find the white rock and the pool spoken of in Father Calanacha's account.

That night, while he was staying in the hut of an Indian, Bingham asked his host the question about the rock and the water. Without hesitation the Indian answered that yes, in a neighboring valley, there was "a great white rock over a spring of water."

It was with a considerable sense of anticipation that Bingham set out with his guides the next morning to find this rock. They found a rock. It was a large white granite boulder that was flattened on the top. Into this boulder there had been carved a sort of seat or platform. At one side of the boulder there was a cave in which there were several carved niches. This cave, Bingham thought, would once have held Inca mummies. But there was no spring of water. The best that he could find was a small irrigation ditch some distance from the white rock. The rock had undoubtedly been a sacred site of some sort for the Incas; such sacred boulders were not uncommon. However, it was not the rock over the spring of water that had made such an impression on Father Calanacha's missionary informants. Another disappointment, yet the area was promising, as all around were signs of the Incas, including terraces and other carved boulders.

Bingham and his guides followed a stream through the thick woods. There in a clearing was "a great white rock." Partially enclosing this boulder were the remains of an Inca temple. But most important of all, one end of the boulder protruded over a pool of running water.

"Since the surface of the little pool, as one gazes at it, does not reflect the sky, but only the overhanging rock, the water looks black and forbidding, even to unsuperstitious Yankees." Here were the very rock and pool described in the Spanish chronicles as a place where the Incas saw the Devil appear as a "visible manifestation." It must have looked black and forbidding to the Spanish as well. This was a place where the followers of the last Incas came to offer gifts and sacrifices.

Bingham described the scene.

It was late on the afternoon of August 9, 1911, when I first saw this remarkable shrine. Densely wooded hills rose on every side. There was not a hut to be seen, scarcely a sound to be heard, an ideal place for practicing the mystic ceremonies of an ancient cult. . . .

We may imagine the sun priests, clad in their resplendent robes of office, standing on the top of the rock at the edge of its steepest side, their faces lit by the rosy light of the early morning, awaiting the moment when the Great Divinity should appear above the eastern hills and receive their adoration. As it rose we may imagine them saluting it and crying: "O Sun! Thou who art in peace and safety, shine upon us, keep us from sickness, and keep us in health and safety. O Sun! Thou who has said let there be Cuzco and Tampu grant that these children may conquer all other people. We beseech thee that thy children the Incas may be always conquerors since it is for this that thou has created them."

Bingham found that, though the Incas and their sun worship were long gone, the shrine was still venerated as a holy place by the Indians who lived in the vicinity. The Indians no longer knew why the rock and pool were sacred; they just knew they were holy and always had been. Once again Hiram Bingham was made aware of the power that the long-dead Incas still held over the land they had once ruled.

With this discovery Bingham was now reasonably certain that he had identified the Vitcos of the chronicles as the ruined fortress on the "Hill of the Roses." But he was not at all certain that this Vitcos was the sole or even the principal capital and hiding place of Manco II and the other last Incas. The confusion of names and places allowed for the possibility that there were really two capitals. Vitcos, the place he had now found, was a relatively accessible city. It was a place where Manco and his successors would have met visitors from the outside world. It was where Manco would have entertained the Spanish deserters. Bingham even thought he found a level place where Manco might have played the game of horseshoes with the Spanish renegades that so unaccountably ended in his death. This fortress would have been the sanctuary that was overrun by the troops of Viceroy Toledo when Inca resistance was finally crushed. But was it the Inca's only sanctuary? Bingham was convinced that it was not, and that there were further discoveries to be made.

In addition to Vitcos, the chronicles also spoke of a city called Vilcapampa. As Bingham pondered the enigmatic and confusing references in the Spanish chronicles, he decided that Vitcos was not Vilcapampa, and that the real Vilcapampa was not only Manco's principal capital but also his secret capital. Vitcos was the place that could be shown to outsiders, but the true source of Manco's power, the home of the Inca religion as well as the Inca's last possible refuge in time of danger, was the unknown

Vilcapampa. So Bingham set out once again into the jungle to find another lost city.

This time the search led him to places that were quite literally off the map. At one point, while crossing the mountains, Bingham looked out in the distance and saw another chain of snowcapped mountains. He had no idea what mountains they were, and he quickly searched his maps, the best available at that time, for the name of this range. These mountains did not exist on the maps, even though the maps were less than a year old. The more he consulted the maps, the more puzzled he became. If the maps were correct, he should, at that moment, have been in the middle of a roaring river, when he was actually "on top of a lofty mountain pass surrounded by high peaks and glaciers."

The mystery was finally solved by the expedition's chief topographer, who figured out that there was an error and some thirty miles between rivers had simply been left off all previous maps. Bingham noted,

> Our surveys opened an unexplored region *15000 square miles in extent*, whose very existence had not been guessed before 1911. It proved to be one of the largest undescribed . . . areas in South America. Yet it is less than a hundred miles from Cuzco, the chief city of the Peruvian Andes, and the site of a university for more than three centuries. That this region could have so long defied investigation and exploration shows better than anything else how wisely Manco had selected his refuge.

In this unexplored land modern trails completely disappeared. Bingham and his party found themselves using ancient paths that had been in use since the days of the

Incas and perhaps earlier. It was raining practically all of the time, which did not improve the condition of the already treacherous trail. "We could see but little of the deep canyon which opened below us and into which we now began to descend four thousand feet through the clouds by a very steep, zigzag path to the hot tropical valley."

On the floor of the valley, the path through the dense jungle became so narrow that Bingham decided "not even a dog could follow it unassisted." The party inched its way forward, crawling over rocks and along slippery cliffs. The heat and humidity were so overpowering that the progress was agonizingly slow and uncomfortable. On August 13, there was a new danger, an earthquake. The region was frequently shaken by earthquakes. This was not a particularly serious one, so the quake didn't bother Bingham. However, it sent the Indians rushing out of shelters in which they were sleeping. The Indians were not cowards: it was force of habit for them. They were used to living in huts with stone walls and tile roofs. Even a mild quake could bring such structures crashing down on the heads of those inside.

In this wild and uncharted region Bingham found himself chasing ghosts. He had heard from several sources of fine ruins at a place called Espiritu Pampa, or "Pampa of Ghosts." Espiritu Pampa was located in a region that had an extremely ominous reputation, and none of the local Indians would willingly go off in search of the place. When they were asked if they wished to work as bearers for the expedition, they would always plead that they were "busy" or that their "crops needed attention" or that their "family could not spare them." The job of carrying supplies through the jungle was not one that the Indians relished anyway, and to carry them into this wild, unknown, and quite possibly dangerous region was a task to be avoided at all costs.

Condore and Mogrovejo, two Peruvian guides who accompanied the expedition, had to round up bearers through a combination of trickery and blackmail. When they found an Indian working on his farm, they would smile in the friendliest possible fashion and walk toward him, hand outstretched, in order to shake hands in the traditional Indian manner. But instead of shaking, they would press a silver dollar into the surprised man's palm. The man was then informed that he had accepted his pay, and he must now do the work. Over the centuries the Indians had learned the hard way that they must be paid in advance or they might not be paid at all. But once they had accepted pay, their own customs as well as the law bound them to carrying out the obligations they had incurred. Protest against this obvious trick proved to be useless, and in a short time half a dozen unwilling carriers had been rounded up.

In addition to the vague and general fears of entering an unknown region and the ominous reputation of Espiritu Pampa, the Indians had a more specific fear of the area into which Bingham now proposed to venture. It was inhabited by the very savage Indians of the Campa tribe, who used poisoned arrows and were very hostile to strangers invading their territory. These Indians were said to acknowledge only the authority of one Saavedra, who was, according to Bingham's informants, "a very powerful man having many Indians under his command and living in grand state with fifty servants, not at all desirous of being visited by anyone."

But the informants also acknowledged that if anyone in the entire region knew of Inca ruins it would be this

Saavedra. So Bingham was both intrigued and unsettled when he realized that in order to do any more successful searching he would first have to find the notorious Saavedra and gain his cooperation.

On the afternoon of August 14, 1911, Bingham found himself in the midst of a dense jungle, "surrounded by tree ferns, vines, and tangled thickets, through which it was impossible to see for more than a few feet." The guides told him to stop, for he was now in the land of the savages who would obey only Saavedra. The guide suggested that perhaps an envoy should be sent on ahead to tell the savages that they were coming on a friendly mission. The envoy who was chosen was not at all happy about his task. He started out slowly and cautiously and was almost immediately lost to sight in the dense undergrowth.

The next half hour or so was a nervous time for Hiram Bingham and the other members of the expedition. They wondered whether they would suddenly be greeted by a hail of poisoned arrows from unseen attackers in the jungle. Bingham tried to form some sort of a mental picture of the mighty Saavedra, sitting in barbaric splendor among his servants and fierce retainers.

> Suddenly we were startled by a crackling of twigs and the sound of a man running. We were instinctively holding our rifles a little higher in readiness for whatever might befall—when there burst out of the woods a pleasant faced young Peruvian *mestizo*, quite conventionally clad, who had come in haste from Saavedra, his father, to extend to us a most cordial welcome! It seemed scarcely credible, but a glance at his face showed that there was no ambush in store for

us. It was with a sigh of relief that we realized there
was to be no shower of poisoned arrows from impenetrable thickets.

The young man led them through a jungle that
gradually became deeper and darker until quite suddenly
it opened up into a field of sugarcane! A few minutes
later they stood in front of the modest hut of Saavedra
himself. There was no crowd of servants and fierce retainers; there were only Saavedra, his wife and children,
and a rather wild-eyed maid who Bingham decided was
the only "savage" around. Saavedra was an extremely
pleasant and helpful fellow, a frontiersman and farmer,
not a warlord. Bingham was very glad that he had not
allowed himself to be frightened off by the rumors of
danger.

Over a meal of boiled chicken, rice, and sweet cassava, Saavedra told Bingham and his companions what
he knew of the ruins at Espiritu Pampa. The "Pampa of
Ghosts," he said, was the location of an Indian village,
and there were extensive ruins beyond the village. But
the trail to these ruins was so difficult that most of it had
to be navigated on hands and knees.

Certainly the Incas had been in this region, for as
Bingham toured Saavedra's land he found that the farmer
was using jars that had been made by the Incas for making his own crude sugar. Saavedra said that he had
found the jars in the jungle. He also showed Bingham
bronze Inca axes that he had dug up on his land. "The
bronzes and the pottery eloquently told us, beyond the
peradventure of a doubt, that Incas had once lived down
here in this damp jungle."

Bingham was eager to push onward, and the next
day, guided by Saavedra's son, he entered the Indian

village of Espiritu Pampa. Here lived the "savages" that Bingham and his companions had worried about so much. In searching for Inca ruins, Bingham had come from the chilly Andean highlands to the lowland jungles. Here in the jungle the people had never acknowledged the rule of the Incas—even though the last of the Incas had lived among them. These jungle Indians lived primarily by hunting and often wore no clothes. The sudden appearance of a naked Indian carrying a bow and arrows startled Bingham. These Indians were, by the definition of the time, savages. And they were suspicious of and hostile to strangers for good reason. The strangers were often thugs from the rubber plantations who would kidnap Indians to work as rubber gatherers, a task which the free-spirited hunters detested. But these "savages" knew and trusted Saavedra, and were more than eager to help any friend of their friend.

As Bingham wandered about the little village, he found more Inca pottery, still another indication that this land had been a refuge for the last of the Incas.

Naturally, the Indians knew of additional ruins in the jungle and offered to guide Bingham to them. Bingham had a difficult time keeping up with the Indians, who seemed able to run through the jungle barefooted and with ease. The heavily booted Bingham tripped and stumbled but somehow managed to keep his fast-moving guides in sight. The hard scramble was amply rewarded when, "hidden behind a curtain of hanging vines and thickets so dense we could not see more than a few feet in any direction the savages showed us the ruins of a group of Inca stone houses whose walls were still standing in fine condition." Here was solid evidence of an extensive Inca settlement.

As the thick jungle vegetation was cleared from the

ruins, Bingham was startled by the size and excellent state of preservation of these ruins. Moreover the Indians themselves seemed surprised at what was being uncovered. Bingham commented that "nothing gives a better idea of the density of the jungle than the fact that the savages themselves had often been within five feet of these fine walls without being aware of their existence."

In just a few short weeks Hiram Bingham had found not just one lost city but three. He had rescued the history of the last four Incas from total obscurity and myth. He had at least tentatively identified most of the major Inca sites mentioned in the chronicles as being connected with Manco and his sons. This hot dense jungle was undoubtedly the place where Titu Cusi, the last of the Incas, was pursued and finally surrendered to the Spanish troops.

The results of Bingham's explorations were fantastic. No one in the history of South American archaeology had ever accomplished so much so quickly, yet Hiram Bingham was strangely unsatisfied. None of the jungle ruins that he had seen truly fulfilled the mental picture that he had built up of Manco's principal city. He envisioned something grander and more mysterious.

In the chronicles Bingham had read that when Manco fled from Cuzco he had taken with him the high priest of the Inca religion and the sacred "Virgins of the Sun." Would they have lived in this hot and steamy valley? Bingham thought not. The difference between Cuzco and Espiritu Pampa was as great as the difference between Scotland and Egypt. "They would not have found . . . the food which they liked. Furthermore, they could have found the seclusion and safety which they craved just as well in several other parts of the province, together with a cool, bracing climate and food stuffs more nearly resembling those to which they were accustomed." He felt that he had not yet identified the place known in the chronicles as "Vilcapampa the old," the principal city of Manco and his sons.

Bingham wanted to go on, but his long-suffering carriers would go no farther. Even the guides complained that they had been away from home too long. Besides, supplies were running low. So the expedition had to turn back. The climb out of the jungle valley back to the heights was a difficult one. "We were soaked with perspiration and drenched with rain. Snow had been falling near the village. Our teeth chattered like castanets." By the time they reached the hut of one of their guides, "[i]t may be doubted whether a more wretched, cold, wet and bedraggled party ever arrived at [the] hut, certainly nothing ever tasted better than that steaming hot sweet tea."

The expedition was not over. Bingham was able to make a few more archaeological discoveries, and he finally got to climb Mount Coropuna, which was a disappointment because it turned out that it wasn't the highest mountain in South America after all. He also got a case of frostbite and severe mountain sickness. There was a lot of mapping of unexplored territory to be done as well. But all the really important discoveries had been made within the first few weeks.

Hiram Bingham had left the United States an unknown; he returned as a famous explorer and a hero. Newspapers and magazines made both Bingham's discoveries and his handsome face familiar to an American public enthralled by adventurous heroes. Still, that failure to identify Manco's principal city, Vilcapampa the old, continued to bother Bingham.

The more he thought about the problem, the more the idea grew that he had actually discovered the city and that it was not in the steamy jungles of the lowlands, but in the mountains. He became convinced that Manco's city was the nameless city that he had found on the mountain called Machu Picchu. As Bingham studied his photographs and notes, and as he read and reread the Spanish chronicles, he began to piece together a fabulous picture of a city so sacred and so secret that its very existence was known only to the Inca himself and to the most important figures in the Inca's sun worship religion. That is why the city's location remained unknown to the Spanish and why even the references to Manco's capital were so confusing. They were confusing because no non-Inca had ever seen the place, none had ever even been near it. Titu Cusi, the last Inca, took the secret of the city with him to his grave.

But grand as all that was, it was only the beginning of Bingham's theory. If the last capital of the Incas was a mystery, the place of origin of the Incas was an even greater mystery. Yet wasn't it logical to assume that the Incas, who were so acutely conscious of their own past, would convert the place from which they had originated into a sacred city?

Hiram Bingham knew that his theory was an extravagant one and that it would not be easily accepted by professional archaeologists in either the United States or South America. He was, after all, an upstart, and in many respects a rank amateur. In order to test his theory, Bingham knew that he was going to have to go back to Machu Picchu. He immediately set about planning another expedition.

Pictures from the Yale Peruvian Expeditions, 1911–1915

Hiram Bingham at Yale.

A typical rough-paved street in Cuzco, which had been the capital of the Inca empire.

Two Peruvian officials of Spanish descent.

Hiram Bingham and his favorite means of transportation.

A breathtaking view of the Urubamba Valley, as seen from
Machu Picchu. The Urubamba River appears in the foreground.

A poste, or post house, in the Peruvian highlands. Bingham and his party stayed in many such places.

Bingham at Machu Picchu in 1915, after the jungle growth was cleared away.

A gateway and one of the numerous stairways at Machu Picchu.
An expedition workman sits on the steps.

The wives of Bingham's guides Richarte and Alvarez stand in front of one of the carefully fitted stone walls of Machu Picchu.

A view of Machu Picchu as it appears today, much as Bingham would have seen it after the heavy vegetation was removed. (Peru National Tourist Office)

CHAPTER 8

"Have I Kept a Single Nugget?"

Hiram Bingham had no trouble finding the money to finance a second expedition to Machu Picchu. Not only did Yale cooperate enthusiastically, but the project also received the support of the prestigious (and well-heeled) National Geographic Society.

The expedition set out in the spring of 1912 and almost immediately ran into enormous difficulties. These difficulties involved getting to Machu Picchu.

It might seem that once a place was "discovered" it would be relatively easy to return to, and usually that's true. In the case of Machu Picchu, however, such logic ignores the almost incredible inaccessibility of the site.

When Bingham had followed Melchor Arteaga to Machu Picchu for the first time, the most frightening and dangerous part of the journey had been crossing the icy, roaring Urubamba River on a jerry-built log bridge. That frail structure had been swept away by the river just a few weeks after Bingham's visit. The climb to the ruins had been difficult enough for Bingham, who had been able to carry all that he needed in the ample pockets of his hunting coat. Bingham had stayed only a couple of days.

In contrast, the 1912 expedition was not intended as a quick visit. The object was to clear the ruins at Machu Picchu and explore the area as thoroughly as possible. This required setting up a camp at the site and provisioning it, so that the explorers, scientists, and workmen could stay for several months. All the supplies would have to be carried up the mountains, and Bingham knew that even the stoutest Quechua would not have been able to carry a very heavy load up the steep trail that he had used.

Richarte and Alvarez, the two Quechuas who lived close to the ruins, often used another trail that ran along the west side of the ridge. Bingham had heard this trail described as "terrifying." Two hardy young members of the expedition tried the trail and found the description all too accurate. They said that the trail was "perilous, winding along the face of rocky precipices and in two or three places crossing in front of sheer rocky cliffs on fragile, rustic ladders." The trail was also much longer. Bingham and the other expedition members decided that it would be impractical, if not impossible, to carry the necessary supplies along such a trail.

Yet the Incas had built a city in this impossible place. They surely must have had an easier way to get to the top. But all signs of the old Inca roads to Machu Picchu had disappeared, and Bingham decided that one of the primary objectives of his expedition would be to locate these ancient roads.

This still left the immediate, practical problem of

setting up and supplying a camp at Machu Picchu. The only solution seemed to be to construct a new bridge across the Urubamba and a new, easier trail to the top. This task Bingham assigned to Kenneth C. Heald, a Colorado mining engineer. Bingham liked Heald because he was a rugged man with a wealth of practical experience and a congenital inability to admit defeat.

Heald had his troubles with poisonous snakes, a fire, and the general difficulty of the terrain. More than once he was nearly killed in a fall. His most alarming experience came when the grass beneath his feet gave way while he was climbing, and he began sliding down the mountain. "For about twenty feet there was a slope of about seventy degrees and then a jump of about two hundred feet after which it would be a bump and [2000 feet] down to the river." As he was sliding, Heald grabbed a bunch of mesquite bush with his right hand. He was going so fast that the resulting jolt tore all the ligaments in his right shoulder, but he held on. It took him nearly half an hour to struggle back to comparatively safe footing. His right arm was by then useless.

Five days later Heald was back on the job, and he tried to make the same climb again, and again he failed. On the third attempt he finally made it. Bingham greatly admired Heald's toughness and determination, and he repeated the story of the engineer's nearly fatal fall practically every time he wrote or spoke of Machu Picchu.

Finding workmen was another chronic problem for the Bingham expedition. The local Quechuas were farmers who disliked carrying loads or clearing jungle; in fact, they generally disliked working for other people. Though the Bingham expedition paid well above prevailing rates paid on the rubber plantations, and the hours of work were much shorter, there were still few willing volunteers. So the government officials—who fully backed the expedition—simply rounded up local Indians and ordered them to work for the expedition. The result was predictable, a group of sullen and unwilling laborers. Bingham understood that the Quechuas were being forced to do the work, and he sympathized with them to a degree. But his reports are filled with complaints about th stubbornness and slowness of the workmen. He was a man in a hurry, and he could not tolerate those who seemed to be standing in his way.

When Hiram Bingham first entered Machu Picchu, he had been awed by the sight. But what he saw then had been at best a partial view, for most of the ruins were obscured by jungle vegetation, which grew in profusion even at that altitude. Walls, even entire buildings, were covered with thorny scrub and bamboo. Clearing the bushes of scrub was no easy task. It was thick and fibrous, and some of it grew so fast that it had to be cut three times in the four months that the expedition spent at Machu Picchu.

Only after the vegetation was cleared and all of the buildings, stairways, and walls were revealed did Bingham fully realize what a wonderful discovery he had made.

The city that we call Machu Picchu—whatever its original inhabitants called it—lies in the saddle between two peaks, Machu Picchu and Huayna Picchu. Surrounding the city itself are agricultural terraces in which the residents were able to grow at least some of their food. Space was extremely limited, so the houses were crammed together, but there was an extensive system of narrow streets and stairways that made getting around the city fairly easy. Bingham found the rock-hewn stairways Machu Picchu's most conspicuous feature. There were over 100 stairways, some quite small but others having as many as 150 steps. Sometimes eight or ten steps were cut from a single boulder.

Attached to many of the houses were tiny garden plots. Once again Bingham was impressed and amazed at the Incas' skillful use of every possible square inch of level space for growing food.

Getting enough water for the inhabitants of the city would have been even a bigger problem than getting enough food. There were some small springs on the side of Machu Picchu mountain, about a mile from the heart of the city. The explorers were able to trace the course of a small conduit from the springs to a series of "fountains" or "basins" in the center of the city. Peruvians call such basins "baths," but Bingham doubted if the Incas did much bathing. "On account of the rarefied air, the cold, and the rapid radiation, even Anglo-Saxons do not bathe frequently in the Peruvian highlands," he observed. Besides, there really wouldn't have been enough water for bathing. The expedition had a great deal of difficulty getting enough water to supply the drinking and cooking needs of a mere forty or fifty people during a four-month period. Bingham wondered if lack of water may not have been one of the reasons the city was abandoned.

Machu Picchu contained private residences and a generous supply of what appeared to be larger public buildings. Bingham thought that most of these large buildings were either royal residences or temples. The most imposing building was one he called the Temple of the Sun because it closely resembled the Temple of the Sun in Cuzco. The temple was the first really fine building that he had seen during his original visit, but only after the walls were cleared of brush and scrubbed clean could Bingham see what a superb structure it was.

"The most experienced master mason of his time had here constructed the most beautiful wall in America," stated the enthusiastic Bingham. He found the Temple of the Sun more pleasing to the eye than the grand marble temples of the Old World. It was sturdier too, for here in a land of frequent earthquakes, where the builders had neither cement nor metal clamps, they had managed to fit the stones together so closely that "there is no place where a pin could be inserted between [them]." They fitted together and held "as tightly as a glass stopper fits into a glass bottle. Friction and an absolutely perfect fit do the trick." The temple walls had withstood the centuries and the ravages of repeated earthquakes.

It was in this temple that Bingham found three windows, which were to play such an important part in his theory of the true identification of Machu Picchu. As he stood before the largest of these windows, he could imagine that it had once been hung with the great golden image of the sun that Manco had rescued from Cuzco and that had been taken from Tupac Amaru, the last of the Incas, when he was captured by the troops of the viceroy Toledo.

As Bingham wandered among the buildings that he called "the King's Group," he imagined how these buildings would have looked when the last Incas lived there. He saw them "fitted with luxurious rugs of vicuna wool as well as the finest blankets and robes that the most skillful of the Chosen Women would weave for the Inca's personal use." These women were enlisted to serve the Inca and the sun god.

What impressed and amazed Bingham, and has had the same effect on practically every visitor to Machu Picchu since, is the prodigious amount of patient labor that must have gone into building the city. Here were people without machines, people who didn't even know how to use a simple pulley. Yet they were able to raise stones weighing many tons to form the tops of doorways, and to cut and fit the stones in walls to within a millimeter of accuracy. The same lavish use of labor and the same care can be found in other Inca constructions, but what makes construction doubly amazing at Machu Picchu was that it was all done at this dizzying height, and often overlooking a sheer drop.

At one point Bingham was trying to take some photographs of a wall from a difficult angle. He had to lean out over a precipice, and he was held by two companions. Bingham, who was rarely bothered by heights, admitted that this time he was "terrified." He began to think about how it would have been to actually build that wall over such a drop, and he was once again struck by a sense of wonder at the skill and daring of the Inca craftsmen.

Machu Picchu was no temporary residence. Clearly people had lived there over a long period of time. That meant that they must also have died there. But where were the bodies buried? Archaeologists often find burials can reveal a great deal about the life of a vanished people.

The Incas didn't usually bury their dead by putting them in a hole in the ground. Most often the Incas arranged the corpse with arms crossed and knees drawn up against the chest, and then wrapped it thoroughly into a compact "mummy bundle." The Incas didn't use any elaborate embalming techniques, as the ancient Egyptians did in preparing their mummies, but in the preservation of a mummy, climate is much more important than embalming. In the arid coastal desert regions of Peru such mummies are almost perfectly preserved, but in the damp highlands of Machu Picchu the mummies would probably be in very poor condition. When the

Inca dead were laid to rest, pottery and other personal objects were generally interred with them. A search of Machu Picchu had turned up only broken pottery, not a single ornament or utensil. It was almost as if the abandoned city had been swept clean, and Bingham began to wonder if they were ever going to learn any more about the builders of the city than could be learned from the silent stones.

Bingham then recalled what he had found at Choqquequirau, the "cradle of gold." At that mountaintop fortress the Incas had placed their dead in burial caves all around the mountain. Bingham instructed his Indian workmen to look for such burial caves, but after a couple of days of searching, they came back and reported they had found nothing. Then Bingham offered a dollar for each cave discovered, and the following day Richarte and Alvarez and their friends reported finding eight caves. The Indians who had come all the way from Cuzco found nothing. Obviously the local Indians had long known of the existence of burial caves, and they had probably done some treasure hunting already. They were just waiting for someone to make them a worthwhile offer before they would reveal their secret.

As it turned out, the mountains around the city of Machu Picchu were dotted with burial caves both natural and artificial. Ultimately nearly one hundred of them were examined by members of the Bingham expedition. Some of the caves contained little more than a rotted bone or two, indicating that they had evidently been entered by either wild animals or treasure hunters. Other caves contained reasonably well preserved mummies as well as pottery, personal ornaments, and sometimes tools.

In examining the caves, one oddity quickly became

apparent. Of those skeletons whose sex could be determined, the vast majority turned out to be women. For example, in a series of caves to which Bingham gave the title Cemetery No. 1, they found the remains of some fifty individuals. Only four of them could be identified as male. About the same percentage held up at other burial sites near Machu Picchu. Bingham found this discovery exciting and significant, for it fitted the theory that he was beginning to formulate. Machu Picchu was really a sacred city, and these female bones were the remains of the Virgins of the Sun or the Chosen Women who served the Inca.

There was no evidence of a royal Inca interment at Machu Picchu. The most elaborate burial found was that of a woman whom Bingham labeled the "High Priestess" or "Mother Superior for the Chosen Women." Close to the bones of this important lady were the bones of a collie-type dog that was bred by the Incas. Some of the woman's personal possessions, including beautifully made pottery, bronze shawl pins, and an unusual and elaborate bronze mirror, were also found.

The tomb of the "High Priestess" was far and away the richest site found at Machu Picchu, yet it contained not a single article of gold. Nor did Bingham find gold of any kind anywhere else at Machu Picchu. The "lost gold of the Incas" was not to be found at Machu Picchu. Later there were those who refused to believe that Bingham had not found a golden treasure, and this was to cause him a great deal of trouble and anguish.

Bingham speculated that the gold the city had once possessed might have been confiscated and sent as part of the ransom for the Inca Atahualpa. Or Tupac Amaru may have taken the remaining gold with him as he fled the city. When the last Inca was captured by the Spanish soldiers, he did have the golden image of the sun and other unspecified treasure of gold with him. All of this was sent to Spain and ultimately melted down to fill the coffers of the Spanish king.

When Bingham examined graves at the fortress that he identified as Vitcos, he found that most of them contained articles of European manufacture. But the graves of Machu Picchu contained virtually nothing that could be assigned to the post-Conquest era. To Bingham this was proof not only that Machu Picchu had never been visited by the Spanish, but that it had never been a permanent residence for the troops of Manco and his sons who would have had opportunities for robbing Spanish travelers. The city was kept entirely free of non-Inca influences. The few post-Conquest items found could easily have been brought by much later travelers who had stumbled upon Machu Picchu but failed to report it. In one cave some beef bones and a couple of peach pits were discovered. Both cows and peaches were unknown to the Incas. These, Bingham thought, were the remains of some later visitor's lunch.

Bingham found that some of the older burial caves contained oddly shaped and colored stones. These he decided were "record stones." He theorized that the stones had different values or meanings and that they were used by the Indians to keep accounts and other records. Some South American Indians as well as people from other cultures in other parts of the world are known to have used such "record stones." However, the Incas were famous for their use of *quipus*, knotted and colored strings for keeping records. According to Bingham's theory the presence of these "record stones" indicated that the Incas had lived at Machu Picchu even before they developed the *quipu* form of record keeping. Machu

Picchu was the only site in Peru where such stones had been found.

Altogether, what Bingham found reinforced his growing belief that the city he found was not only the home of the last Incas but of the first Incas as well, and quite possibly the cradle of Andean civilization.

Once the ruins had been cleared, the next step in Bingham's plan of exploration was to find the Inca highways that led to Machu Picchu. The Incas were great road builders, and it was inconceivable that so important a city would not have been connected to their highway system somehow. Finding these roads was going to be no easy task. Since the location of the city was unknown to the Spanish and was ultimately forgotten by practically everyone, the roads had not been mapped, and they certainly had not been maintained. In dry regions the unmistakable signs of Inca roads would remain visible for centuries, but in this damp region, jungle-choked mountain roads were quickly obliterated, covered by vegetation and washed away by landslides. Bingham started by following the road from the main gate of the city. After a short time the road seemed to divide. The right-hand fork led to the summit of another mountain, while the left-hand fork led to seemingly impassable cliffs.

It wasn't until 1915 that another Bingham expedition was actually able to trace the roads that led to Machu Picchu. "We heard from one of the Indians that there were ruins in a region of high mountains and impassable jungles south of Machu Picchu Mountain. It was tantalizing to think of the possibilities of exploration in a country which in ancient days must have been closely connected with the hidden city." Of all the areas that Bingham visited, this was perhaps the least known. The Spanish conquistadores and their historians never mentioned it. Later explorers hardly touched on it. "It appears to have been a *terra incognita*," Bingham commented. Naturally he had to go there.

Bingham began his exploration of the mysterious region in April of 1915. There were no great hidden cities to be found in this jungle, but Bingham did find the remains of the road he had been looking for, and at convenient intervals along the road were the ruins of Inca way stations or guardhouses. It was a typically efficient Inca highway. To Bingham's satisfaction, this road led directly toward Machu Picchu.

"I had at last achieved my desire of penetrating the unexplored country southeast of Machu Picchu, a region which had tempted me for many years. We had learned a little more of that 'something' which, as Kipling says, was 'lost behind the ranges.'" Bingham's reference was to Rudyard Kipling's 1898 poem "The Explorer." Bingham had become very conscious of himself as an explorer. An explorer had to be tough and brave. Physically Bingham was extremely tough, and even privately he rarely complained of hardships or pain. The explorer, in Bingham's view, had to be well prepared and disciplined, and he should approach his task with a scientific detachment. The explorer was not a conquistador or a treasure hunter—he was out to advance human knowledge and perhaps to satisfy his own curiosity. Bingham was even conscious of how the proper explorer should look, and he carefully cultivated this image. He was most often photographed in full Abercrombie & Fitch regalia: khaki riding britches and shirt, mid-calf leather boots, and a battered khaki hat. He also wore what he called his "useful hunting coat, designed to carry everything."

More than anyone else, the handsome and photogenic Hiram Bingham became the image of the explorer for

Americans. He was the model for the hero of several adventure novels, and Bingham is clearly the inspiration for Indiana Jones, the popular film hero professor-explorer—right down to the battered hat.

Bingham himself didn't actually have the opportunity to connect the road that he had discovered with Machu Picchu. That task he assigned to topographer Clarence Maynard. Maynard was another one of those gritty, determined, and practical men who Bingham liked so much. Just as he enjoyed telling the story of Kenneth Heald's slipping down the mountain, he had a favorite tale about Maynard as well. While tracing the route to Machu Picchu, Maynard was riding his mule along a narrow trail bordered by a drop of several hundred feet. It had been raining and the trail was unusually treacherous. Suddenly the mule slipped and fell to his knees, and in trying to scramble back to his feet seemed about to fall over the edge. Maynard, who had no desire to go over the edge with his mule, threw himself out of the saddle. Maynard's journal noted blandly, "Landed on my back, on a rock. Throwing weight that way evidently righted the mule. He floundered around. His hoofs seemed to be all over me, but he didn't step on me. Managed to roll out of the way. Arrived at camp about eleven thirty." No giving up, no turning back, and no complaints either.

It took Maynard several weeks to connect the two trails, but ultimately he was successful, and Hiram Bingham had the enormous satisfaction of picking up the road where he had to leave it and being able to enter Machu Picchu "over the very road used by the Virgins of the Sun when they fled here from Cuzco and the conquistadors."

Bingham's expedition discovered a number of other roads, and he found that there had once been quite an elaborate system of highways through the unknown and barely populated region. In the time of the Incas the area probably had been densely populated.

By the end of 1915 Bingham was absolutely convinced that Machu Picchu was "Vilcapampa the Old," the principal city of Manco Inca and his sons. He was pleased by the thought that Tupac Amaru, the last Inca, had lived in this city which "surpassed anything his cruel conquerors ever saw or found." Bingham was also pleased that "the Chosen Women lived and died there in peace, unmolested by the Spanish conquerors."

That was only part of Bingham's theory. Machu Picchu had quite clearly not been built by the last Incas, it was quite an old city. But how old, and what were its origins?

The origins of the Incas themselves are rather foggy. Most authorities contend, as did the Incas themselves, that they came from Cuzco, which remained their capital until the time of the Spanish Conquest. As far as the Incas were concerned, history started with them, and little is known of pre-Inca Peru. However, there were a few legends and tales that connect the Incas and their legendary founder, the first Manco Inca, with a place called Tampu Tococo. According to the legends, it was from there that the Incas went forth to conquer Cuzco and the rest of the empire.

There were even older stories about pre-Inca kings called the Amautas, who had ruled Peru for some sixty generations. The last of these kings, Pachacoti VI, goes the story, was killed in battle with savage hordes and his body was spirited away by his surviving troops and hidden in a cave at Tampu Tococo. Many refugees from the disorder of war fled to this secret place.

Roughly translated, Tampu Tococo means "a place

of temporary abode with windows" or "window tavern." The temporary part didn't seem to apply to Machu Picchu, but Bingham thought that the window part most certainly did. There were windows in many of the houses at Machu Picchu, not a common feature of Inca architecture. Then there was the temple with the three windows. Legends also connected such a temple with the birthplace of Manco I. Thus Bingham felt that the name of this fabled city was highly significant.

Bingham believed that he had found enough evidence to identify Machu Picchu with Tampu Tococo, making it both the first and the last capital of the Incas. Bingham also believed that in the eight or ten centuries between the fall of the Amautas and the rise of the Incas, Machu Picchu was the place where "there were kept alive the wisdom, skill, and best traditions of the ancient folk who had developed the civilization of Peru."

After Manco, the first Inca emperor, conquered Cuzco, Machu Picchu was partially deserted and largely forgotten by the common folk. But it had not been abandoned altogether. Its location was certainly known to the priests of the sun and to the Inca himself. It also may have been maintained as the place where the Chosen Women were educated.

Bingham contended that many of the Inca structures in Cuzco had actually been built in imitation of older structures at Machu Picchu, rather than the other way round. When the Incas were driven from Cuzco, it was only natural that they should retreat to this hidden city, which had, a thousand years earlier, served as the final refuge for the last of the Amautas.

In the end, the last Incas soldiers lived and fought in the lowlands, while Machu Picchu became the refuge for the Chosen Women. "Here concealed in a canyon of

remarkable grandeur, protected by nature and the hand
of man, the 'Virgins of the Sun' one by one passed away
on this beautiful mountain top and left no descendants
willing to reveal the importance or explain the
significance of the ruins . . . which crown the beetling
precipices of Machu Picchu."

A fine and romantic vision, especially from a man
who usually tried to portray himself as a hardheaded and
unromantic fellow. It is a vision of ancient kings, hidden
cities, and beautiful women. It is a vision worthy of
popular works of heroic fantasy. Indeed Bingham's writings on Machu Picchu did influence a number of writers
of this sort of fantasy. The writer August Derleth made
Machu Picchu part of the "Cthulhu Mythos," a fictional
cosmology originally developed by the fantasy writer
H. P. Lovecraft. In a Derleth story the evil god Cthulhu
was worshipped near Machu Picchu.

Bingham realized that most American archaeologists
would regard his theory as fantasy as well, and he was
correct. His theory of Machu Picchu as the legendary
Tampu Tocco never had many supporters among the
professionals—it was all too speculative and grand for
cautious scientists and scholars. Even the identification
of Machu Picchu as Manco's Vilcapampa has been seriously questioned. Most authorities now believe that the
real Vilcapampa probably was the fortress that Bingham
found at Espiritu Pampa. So one way or the other,
Hiram Bingham probably did discover the capital of the
last Incas.

If Machu Picchu wasn't Vilcapampa or Tampu
Tocco, what was it? The best guess today is that it was a
citadel, a place of retreat and refuge for the people who
lived in the villages of the Urubamba Valley. In the
earlier days of the Inca empire this area had been, as

Bingham suspected, heavily populated. But it was also dangerously close to an area peopled by unconquered and extremely hostile tribes of the jungle. When these tribes attacked, the villagers could scramble up the road to Machu Picchu and defend themselves by dropping rocks on the heads of the invaders, who could use only a narrow path of approach. There appear to be no defensive walls in Machu Picchu. Its protection was its inaccessible location. Other areas of the Inca empire used such fortresses, but none was built on the scale of Machu Picchu.

This theory does not explain all the problems connected with Machu Picchu. For example, it does not explain why the residents appear to have been mainly women, or why it was abandoned and forgotten. So an air of mystery and wonder still clings to the mountaintop city first discovered by Hiram Bingham in 1911.

By 1915 Bingham's primary problems were not with the jungles or the altitude, but with the Peruvian government. In 1911 and 1912 the government of Peru had warmly supported Bingham's efforts. By 1915 the government had changed, and there was an entirely new and far more suspicious attitude toward Yankee explorers. The new government assumed that Bingham, like the conquistadores, was looking for gold, and in 1915 government officials accused Bingham and the staff of the Yale Peruvian expedition of smuggling gold out of Machu Picchu. Government agents inspected the expedition's shipping crates and filed claims—apparently false—that they contained contraband material.

Bingham was furious. He had carefully cultivated his self-image as the disinterested explorer. He was a scientist who sought out lost civilizations for the advancement of human knowledge and for "his own private improvement and amusement." To be acccused of stealing gold cut to the very heart of this image.

Bingham's attitude was one that the Peruvians could not understand and certainly did not trust. All the other foreigners who had come to Peru were looking for gold or something else to steal. For his part Bingham was incredulous "that our statement that we were members of the National Geographic Society . . . was no claim in consideration." Once again Bingham could have drawn his inspiration from Kipling's explorer. "Have I kept a single nugget . . . No, not I." Bingham didn't find any nuggets and wouldn't have kept any if he had.

Bingham, with his personal integrity under attack, left Peru in a fury. He was deeply wounded, but he tried to cover his feelings by adopting a rather flippant attitude when he told former president Theodore Roosevelt that he then "decided there were pleasanter activities for an American citizen than exploring Peru, and I came home."

Bingham was to continue to think, lecture, and write about Machu Picchu. Though it was to remain the keystone of his fame, he was not to return there for more than thirty years. Bingham did not immediately realize how seriously this accusation of treasure hunting was to affect his life. Within a few months of his return, he was caught up in a new enthusiasm. War was being fought in Europe, and to Bingham it seemed only a matter of time, and not very much time, before the United States would be embroiled in the war. Bingham didn't oppose the war; indeed, he thought it was America's duty to fight. His only anxiety was that at the age of forty-one he would not be able to see the sort of action that he craved.

The role of the foot soldier in World War I was dreary. The cavalry, which would once have attracted a man of adventure like Bingham, was obsolete in mechanized warfare. There was only one area in which the true adventurer could flourish—Hiram Bingham decided to become an aviator.

CHAPTER 9

"Like a Knight of Old"

W hen Hiram Bingham decided to become an aviator, not only had he never flown a plane before, he also had never even been in one. Of course, back in 1917 the airplane was still quite new, so most people had never been in a plane before. Over in Europe airplanes were already being used in the war, but the United States still had no air force. Indeed, the nation had not produced a single military airplane. Many in America, including many in the army, thought the airplane was a military fad or at the very least far too unreliable a piece of machinery to make an effective weapon of war. Bingham disagreed, and in this case he was to be proved spectacularly correct.

What particularly attracted Bingham to flying were the reports of the daring exploits of European "flying aces" that appeared in all the newspapers. The dashing aviators who flew above the nameless foot soldiers in the trenches were considered real heroes.

Early in 1917 Bingham discussed the possibility of learning to fly with the American aviation pioneer Glenn Curtiss. Curtiss told him that anyone who could ride a horse or sail a boat could learn to fly. Bingham had done some sailing, and though he had not done a great deal of horseback riding, he had spent an awful lot of time on mules—so he figured he could learn to fly.

Curtiss estimated that in 1917 there were probably fewer than twenty-five qualified flying instructors in the entire United States. Several of them worked at a flying school that Curtiss ran in Miami, Florida. So early in March 1917, Bingham arrived at the Curtiss school in Miami ready to learn how to fly. He found his first trip in a plane as a passenger "almost enjoyable." He was in the front seat of an open two-seater plane, where the wind and the roar of the engine made the trip uncomfortable and disorienting. But he was not discouraged by the experience. Nor was he in the least discouraged by the dangers involved in learning to fly. The Curtiss school, as Curtiss was the first to admit, was a mess. The planes were old, and many had been poorly designed in the first place. They had been repaired repeatedly, often by people who didn't quite know what they were doing, using parts that didn't really fit properly. These planes were held together by spit and baling wire.

To this should be added the fact that most of the instructors were inexperienced and still were pushing students through the course as quickly as possible because they were all convinced that America would soon be in the war and would need pilots. So it is not hard to understand why there were frequent accidents at the school. Bingham recalled: "Connecting rods broke in mid-air and frightened new pilots by smashing holes in crank cases. Roger Jannus went up one day and while turning a loop had the novel experience of having his propeller fly to pieces." Somehow he managed to land safely.

Shortly before he was to make his own first solo flight
Bingham witnessed an even more spectacular accident:

> One day a newly assembled plane, the wings of
> which were not exactly of the same pattern, was
> piloted by an inexperienced teacher who had with
> him a new pupil on his first or second flight. They got
> into a tail spin and fell over 1500 feet making a com-
> plete crash. The engine was partially buried in the
> ground, and the plane was so flattened out that
> hardly any of it was more than a foot above the sur-
> face. It seemed like a miracle that neither one of the
> occupants was killed. Both of them were out of the
> hospital and hobbling around in about ten days.

Did that scare Bingham? Not at all. "It gave us more
confidence to see what might happen without a fatal end-
ing."

After a few days of instruction Bingham was deemed
ready to take a plane out on his own. "My first solo flight
was made in an old ship that had turned over on its back
twice within the previous 48 hours." The mechanics
didn't quite know what was wrong with the plane, but
they fiddled over it for a while, made a few adjustments,
and declared it fit to fly. If going up in this flying junk
heap worried Bingham, he certainly wouldn't admit it.
He said only that he was glad enough to get the chance to
fly at all.

"The motor started off well and I had attained some
little altitude after flying for about seven minutes when
the motor unaccountably stopped." Bingham contem-
plated gliding back to a landing but recalled that on the
previous day a student had done just that and had been
severely criticized for not restarting his engine in the air.

So Bingham tried switching the engine on and off, and in a little while it would catch briefly. He would go a little farther and the engine would die again. Finally Bingham tired of this game of on and off, and he brought the balky plane in for a hard landing in the sand in front of the runway. This was considered a moderately successful first solo flight, and Bingham was elated. Within the month he had earned his pilot's license.

The United States declared war on Germany on April 6, 1917, and Bingham enlisted immediately. He applied for and received a commission in the aviation section of the Signal Officer Reserve Corps. Bingham wanted to get into combat flying, so he first went to Canada, where he visited an air field in Toronto that had served as a training base for Canadians and for some Americans who had gone to war before their country actually did. He greatly admired the almost foolhardy courage of these young aviators.

In November, Bingham was called back to the United States and put in charge of "Air Personnel" for the new U.S. Air Service. His office was not on the front lines as he had hoped, but in Washington, D.C., and he hated it. He felt he had been "chained to a desk" when he would much rather have been "in camp or out-of-doors." He had not risked his neck in broken-down planes to get a desk job.

When Bingham came to Washington, he found the fledgling air service in a state of nearly total chaos. There were hundreds of clerks jammed into a huge barnlike building, but few seemed to know what they were supposed to do. People kept running in and out on unaccountable but distracting errands. It took hours or even days to find the proper files, and sometimes the files were never found at all.

The United States was generally unprepared for its entry into World War I, and Bingham felt that the air service was in even worse shape than the rest of the military. He was horrified by some of the official absurdities. Officers in the air service, he noted, were required to wear spurs with their full dress uniforms. Even in the cavalry, horses were becoming a rarity, but for an aviator to wear spurs! The always image-conscious Bingham was indignant when British and Canadian aviators laughed at the Americans for their wings and spurs. The uniform of the aviator, Bingham declared, was fine for fighting on the ground, but its cut severely restricted a pilot's arms and made operating a plane uncomfortable. Aviators needed their own uniforms, not something designed for another service. Bingham frequently repeated the story of the cavalry officer who was promoted into the air service and who insisted on having a hitching post set up in his office. It was an anecdote he laced with humor and scorn.

Bingham was ambitious, and consciously or not he had chosen a branch of the military that was not filled with career officers who might block his path to promotion. There were plenty of officers in the air service, just not many good ones. Bingham had nothing but contempt for most of the officers because they didn't know how to fly, and he thought they were afraid to learn how. Bingham had a long litany of complaints against these "non flying officers," and he said privately and then after the war publicly that all of them should retire from the air service and should leave the way open for officers like himself who were at least trained pilots. He was beginning to show flashes of the lack of tact that was to get him into a lot of trouble in the years to come.

Though Bingham certainly enjoyed the prospect of

moving up rapidly in the military, he was no mere opportunist. He genuinely wanted to go out and fight "the Huns"—as the Germans were invariably called during World War I. He was ready and eager to risk his life on what he regarded as a "holy crusade." He wrote to his wife that as during the time of the Crusades, there was "no time for thinking of the future. I am on the altar, whether I be consumed or not is for fate to decide." No one could ever question Hiram Bingham's great physical courage—he was ready to fight and die. However, he certainly wasn't going to be "consumed" in Washington by anything other than frustration and boredom. Bingham kept badgering his superior officers as well as his high-placed friends to get him out of Washington and over to Europe where the fighting was being done. Finally, early in 1918 he was sent to France, but not as a combat aviator, because though Bingham hated to admit it, he was both too old and too inexperienced to take on that role. The "air aces" either were young men or were older men who had been flying for years. Bingham was to help organize the training of American aviators in France. His prior career as a teacher as well as his present role as an aviator helped to influence the decision to give him that position. He complained that he wouldn't get a chance to fly in combat, but at least he was out of the office and in a camp where he could mix with adventurous and active men like himself.

There was a notion among many in the military that the pilot was little more than a flying chauffeur, not a real officer at all. This Bingham rejected vigorously. "The pilot is more like the knight of old or the modern cavalry officer. He must first of all be . . . an officer and a gentleman." Later, Bingham discovered that he had overstated the case a bit, for many of the American pilots may have been officers, but they were not gentlemen.

Almost a year after he had made his first flight, Hiram Bingham set out for France to take up his duties as chief of personnel for the air service in the city of Tours. The crossing was made aboard the *Aquitania*, a passenger liner hurriedly converted to troop ship. It was a large and not very maneuverable vessel crammed with American men and equipment bound for Europe to fight the Germans. It would have been a perfect target for the German U-boats patrolling the Atlantic. Aboard the *Aquitania* the rumor spread that the ship was being stalked by a U-boat. Everybody had to wear life preservers at all times. When the *Aquitania* actually entered the combat zone it began making all sorts of evasive zigzag movements. The ship had not been designed for that sort of activity, and everything on board began sliding or crashing around. Practically everybody on board was made horribly seasick by the rolling and pitching motion. There were also several submarine scares when the gunners on the *Aquitania* began firing at what they took to be the conning tower of a German U-boat. But this was all the product of anxiety, for no U-boats were actually sighted and the ship landed safely after what Bingham, with characteristic understatement, called "a fairly exciting passage."

Waiting for Bingham in France were some 1,800 young flying cadets. They had enlisted with great enthusiasm and had received some training in the United States before being shipped off to France for further training on combat aircraft. But there were no training facilities available for them, and the flying cadets sat around for months with little to do except get into trouble. In fact, the cadets had picked up a rather notorious reputation in France. They were, in Bingham's words, "the class of young, irresponsible, venturesome, athletic boys who were willing to take the risk of aviation training when about four percent of all advanced students were killed in training. They felt they were gambling their lives every time they went up." And indeed they were. They were a wild lot, yet Bingham liked them all very much. He called the treatment that these flying cadets had received in France "the worst page in the history of the Air Service."

Bingham's career in the air service flourished. He rose to the rank of lieutenant colonel and finally was put in command of the U.S. flight training base at Issoudun in France, the largest Allied flight training base in Europe. Bingham was a wonderful organizer and teacher, and his enthusiasm for flying inspired everyone he met. At Issoudun young pilots were schooled in the use of new equipment and in the rapidly changing techniques of aerial combat. The sort of fatalistic cheerfulness that reigned at Issoudun was reflected in this notice that was posted around the base: "Do not overshoot the field as you will only crash and will not learn anything."

Issoudun was supposed to provide a refresher course for the cadets before they were sent to the front. Instructors were drawn from that small elite of World War I flying aces. Captain Eddie Rickenbacker was the engineering officer at Issoudun. The Americans were also trained by European fliers who were really more experienced in aerial combat. One of them, a Royal Air Force (RAF) ace named Captain Armstrong, made a strong impression on Bingham with a spectacular arrival. In his book *An Explorer in the Air Service*, Bingham described the scene:

> One day I was crossing the street from my quarters to my office when the unaccustomed sound produced by a plane looping near the ground called my attention to the extraordinary antics of a Sopwith Camel. It made loop after loop over the headquarters, missing the roofs of the building by only a few feet, finally coming so close to the ground as to cause us all to hold our breath as the marvelously skillful pilot pulled his ship out of a loop within a few inches of the ground, fairly touching the long grass. Then the machine was pulled straight up into a 'zoom' of unparalleled magnitude. It stalled, fell like a leaf, fluttering from side to side, recovered, made a tight spiral incredibly near the ground, lit as gracefully as a butterfly and hardly rolled more than a few inches. Then a small dog bounded out of the cockpit from the pilot's lap to the ground, while the pilot himself with a novel under his arm and a smile on his face walked nonchalantly across the airdrome. Thus did Captain Armstrong announce his arrival.

Later, when writing about Captain Armstrong, Bingham felt compelled to say that while the kind of stunt flying that he did was encouraged by the RAF among its pilots it was very much frowned upon by the U.S. Air Service, because it was unnecessary and much too dangerous. Armstrong himself was killed, not in combat, for he had come to Issoudun just days before the end of the war, but shortly after the armistice while flying similar stunts too close to a hangar. Yet Bingham could hardly contain his admiration for this recklessly daring man, and called Captain Armstrong "the most graceful and skillful flyer I have ever seen."

Armstrong was to teach "night pursuit" to the American cadets. This was a technique that he had developed to such a fine skill that he declared it almost "not sporting" to shoot down an enemy plane during such an encounter. However, Armstrong never really got a chance to teach his technique to the Americans. A week after he arrived, the armistice was signed. Bingham described the reaction of the American pilots who were to learn night pursuit as one of "bitter disappointment."

It is hard to escape the impression that the armistice, which was welcomed throughout the world as marking the end to the most terrible war that had been fought to that time, was a bitter disappointment to Hiram Bingham as well.

Bingham never did get his chance to "fly over the lines" and engage in aerial combat. In fact, he only went to the front lines once, and that was in July 1918 on an inspection tour of the battlefield at Château-Thiery— scene of one of the bloodiest battles of the war. The heavy fighting was over before Bingham arrived. It was his job to assess the value of aircraft and reconnaissance balloons in the battle.

He never tried to pass himself off as a war hero, though simply going up in a training plane during World War I was quite dangerous, and Bingham had survived several harrowing crashes. He rarely spoke of his own perils, but when pressing for increased pay for those who trained military pilots, he recounted the fate of his own instructors.

"My first instructor in an Army machine was killed in the course of a practice combat dive." The second instructor was killed "while giving a lesson in spiralling to the pupil whose turn immediately preceded mine." The pupil in this case was seriously injured. His third instructor survived the rigors of training and managed to make it to aerial combat at the front, which he also survived. Bingham's fourth instructor was less lucky. He was killed trying to bring a plane out of a dangerous position in which it had been thrown by an inexperienced student. "My fifth instructor and the one who succeeded by his patience and skill in giving me a sense of confidence in the tricky Niquport 23 [was] killed by being thrown from his machine while diving at a target." And as Bingham pointed out, these men were "not beginners or poorly trained pilots but experts in the art of flying."

Just as he had refused to complain too much about the hardships and dangers of exploration and mountain climbing, Bingham thought that it was the mark of the true aviator not to dwell upon the dangers or to brag about any successes. Another RAF aviator that Bingham admired greatly was Colonel L. W. B. Rees, who had single-handedly routed ten German warplanes. "It was only with the greatest difficulty that one could get Colonel Rees to speak of his great fight, even in private."

Yet if Bingham would not complain of hardship and danger he had no qualms at all about heaping scorn on those "sham airmen" who he felt were afraid to fly themselves and were blocking progress for the air service. When his book *An Explorer in the Air Service* came out in 1920 reviewers were impressed by his knowledge of flying, but some were taken aback by the stinging tone of his criticisms.

Bingham stayed in France until Christmas 1918 and then returned to Washington for a few months to tie up some loose ends about the air service wartime training. In March 1919, Lieutenant Colonel Hiram Bingham retired, with many honors, from the U.S. Air Service.

Once again a civilian, Bingham wasn't sure what he was going to do with the rest of his life. He had not really planned beyond the end of the war. While many men who returned from the war wanted nothing more than to spend time with their families, that was not Hiram Bingham's desire. The old Bingham wanderlust gripped him again. Being a very rich civilian, he was able to wander in style. He took an extended sailing trip in the Pacific, spending much of his time in his native Hawaii. He discovered that the Bingham name still carried considerable weight among a certain segment of the native population of the islands, and on his return to the islands he was welcomed with enthusiastic demonstrations. He was touched, particularly since his childhood in Hawaii had been lonely and unhappy. In a letter to his wife he confessed, "It does not seem possible that I am related to that little friendless boy who incurred the wrath of the Adult population for trying to run away from home in 1888, and the scorn of the youthful part of Honolulu for failing to Succeed."

The Hiram Bingham of the 1920s was neither friendless nor unsuccessful. He had already successfully pursued three careers as scholar, explorer, and aviator. When he returned from his trip, he decided that he would try a fourth career, politics, and since he now had plenty of powerful friends in Connecticut, he knew that he was not going to have to start at the bottom.

CHAPTER 10

"Senators I Understand Not at All"

Hiram Bingham was a political leader's dream candidate. Even before television, a candidate's appearance was important, and Bingham was handsome, though with more lines on his face and his hair a glorious silver he could more properly be called distinguished-looking. Bingham was certainly well educated, wealthy, and socially prominent. He was a college teacher with a fine war record and considerable fame as an explorer. He had an impressively large family of seven sons. All in all, he exemplified those "manly virtues" that were so prized by politicians of the 1920s.

Throughout the 1920s, Connecticut was a devoutly Republican state, and the politics were controlled by one man, J. Henry Roreback. Though the seat of Roreback's power was the rural areas of the state, he was a true political boss in every sense of the word. Roreback chose the Republican candidates for the state and the voters

dutifully elected them. Bingham had already been involved in Republican politics in Connecticut and was
therefore well known to Roreback. So when Bingham
returned from his voyage somewhat at loose ends and
expressed an interest in running for public office, "Boss"
Roreback immediately saw the advantage of such a candidate and picked him to run for lieutenant governor in
1922.

Bingham won with ease. The job of lieutenant governor is not a particularly important or influential one.
Indeed, the job is largely irrelevant unless the governor
happens to die in office. It is generally considered a political launching pad, and with his big electoral win, Bingham's political career was very well launched. He
planned to go on to become governor and eventually
U.S. senator, and that's what he did, but much more
quickly and in a more unorthodox fashion than anyone
had imagined.

In November 1924, Bingham ran for governor of
Connecticut and won in a landslide, carrying every electoral district in the state. However, late in October one
of Connecticut's U.S. senators, Frank Brandegee, committed suicide, and a special election was held to fill
Brandegee's seat. Though he had not yet been inaugurated as governor, Hiram Bingham, with Roreback's
full backing, decided to run for senator. He was bitterly
criticized in some quarters as being overly ambitious.
"Double Dip" Bingham, he was called by the papers.
Bingham ignored the criticism and the public did too, for
they handed him another big victory. He thus had landslide victories in two statewide elections for two different
offices in less than two months. That is some sort of a
political record in America.

Bingham's rather bizarre situation raised a host of

legal questions. Could he resign as governor before he had actually been inaugurated? Bingham decided that he couldn't, so in January 1925 he was officially inaugurated, and he threw one of the biggest, most lavish inaugural balls the state or the nation had ever seen. Two days later he resigned to take his seat in the U.S. Senate.

The new senator from Connecticut was immediately recognized by the press as a man to watch. "Keep an eye on Bingham as his Senate career progresses," wrote Reuban Maury in *Liberty* magazine. "He is one of the most striking figures in the Senate." After his election the press frequently mentioned what a good-looking senator he was.

Because of his experience with the air service, he was put on committees dealing with aviation, and he became one of the more forceful spokesmen for the promotion of air power in the United States. He was dubbed "The Flying Senator," a title that he lived up to. Once he raced to make an important Senate vote in a U.S. Army blimp, landing in the Capitol plaza before a hastily assembled but delighted crowd of reporters and photographers. "That's the way all congressmen will arrive in the future," he announced.

On another occasion he flew an autogyro—the forerunner of the helicopter—from the Capitol plaza to his country club in Virginia. He touted the autogyro as the family plane of the future. A photograph of Bingham, wearing his flying helmet with his golf clubs slung over his shoulder as he boarded the craft, appeared in newspapers and magazines all over the country. He also landed his autogyro on the White House lawn.

Another news photo showed Bingham as best man at the wedding of one Porter Adams, a forgettable photo except that it also shows the maid of honor at this wedding was the famed aviator Amelia Earhart. When Charles Lindbergh came to Washington, Bingham was seen and photographed by his side. He could not be ignored.

Although Hiram Bingham was not the most effective, or even attentive, of senators, his senatorial career, particularly in its early years, had real virtues. His unique life had given him expertise in areas unknown to most politicians. He knew more about flying than anyone else in Congress, and he appreciated the enormous potential of both military and commercial aviation. He could speak with great authority about South America and Hawaii and other U.S. interests in the Pacific. He had the potential to be an enormously valuable legislator. But the very qualities that had made him a successful explorer and fine air service officer created problems for him in politics. He craved action and movement, even danger. Sitting around reading reports was an activity that he had little patience for. Both in the field as an explorer and during the war he was used to commanding, not politicking and compromising. He didn't really understand how the business of politics was carried out, and he didn't really want to.

In the Senate, Bingham never became "one of the boys" or part of the inner circle of that body. On the contrary, he often expressed a kind of lofty scorn for ordinary "politicians" and their ways. Those politicians, who saw Bingham grabbing headlines and always having his picture taken, resented his attitude. This resentment was to grow and was ultimately to cause Hiram Bingham a great deal of trouble. But whatever the other senators might have thought of Bingham, the voters of Connecticut certainly liked their "Flying Senator." In 1926, when he ran for a full term, he was reelected by a vote of 183,613 to 104,037, another landslide.

Bingham was not going to allow himself to be chained to a desk in either Washington or Connecticut. In 1925 he went back to South America, though not to Peru, and led an expedition that climbed Mount Coropuna once again. At age fifty, Hiram Bingham was remarkably fit. In 1927 he became one of the first U.S. senators to take an extensive foreign trip. He went to the South Pacific.

In 1929 he crossed the Pacific once again, and during his trip he stopped at Hawaii. This time his reception was even more enthusiastic than it had been in 1919. Bingham was hailed by practically everyone in the islands as Hawaii's most famous native son, and he picked up another nickname, "the Senator from Hawaii." Once again it was a title that he had earned; not merely had he been born in Hawaii, but he had always promoted the interests of the islands.

In his 1929 trip Bingham got as far as China, which was at that time in the middle of its long and brutal civil war between the Nationalists and the Communists. While he was in Peking, he became involved in the case of a woman named Mrs. Michal Borodin. She was the wife of a Soviet official, and she had been arrested by the Nationalists and was about to be executed for distributing Communist propaganda. Hiram Bingham was a conservative Republican—he was about as rigidly anti-Communist as anyone in the Senate. He had no reservations whatever about executing revolutionaries. Yet Hiram Bingham, the gallant adventurer, could not allow a woman to be executed without trying to do something about it.

He confronted the Nationalist leader in Peking,

Chang Tso-lin, and told him that if the execution went ahead the Nationalists would be regarded as "brutal and barbaric"—strong words from a visiting senator. Chang merely shrugged and reminded Bingham that he had already executed twenty Communists on the previous day and was ready to execute twenty more. But in the face of Bingham's total disapproval, Chang relented: "You Westerners are so foolish about your women. I won't execute her, but that's what she deserves." It's hard to imagine that this widely publicized incident did not serve as an inspiration for scenes in *Shanghai Express* and other "China films" that were to become popular Hollywood fare during the 1930s.

In the days before jet travel, trips to Asia and South America could take months, and Bingham spent a lot of time away from his desk in Washington—as much time away as possible. Bingham was probably the most well-traveled man in the Senate. In those days the matter of congressional travel was really no issue. Bingham's constituents certainly didn't seem to object to his trips. He could easily, and correctly, have defended his travels by pointing out that now that the United States had become a world power it was vital that members of Congress know more about the world. But since his travels were not criticized, he never felt the need to defend them.

When he was in Washington, he did do some work in areas other than aviation, South America, and territories like Hawaii. One of the major issues in Congress in 1929 was the question of tariffs, that is, taxes on foreign goods brought into the country. Bingham had on his Senate payroll a man named Charles Eyanson, who was also a paid clerk of the Connecticut Manufacturers Association. Bingham brought Eyanson into closed meetings of the tariff committee. He also asked Eyanson to help draft parts of the tariff bill affecting the future of Connecticut industry. Eyanson's activities represented a clear conflict of interest. If such a conflict was not precisely illegal, it was definitely against the established customs of the Senate, and when Eyanson's affiliation with the Connecticut Manufacturers Association became known, there was an uproar.

At first Bingham tried to brush aside the criticism, insisting that he had done nothing wrong and that others had done the same. But as the criticism persisted and grew harsher, he reacted with unconcealed anger. A Senate hearing was called to look into Bingham's activities, and when Bingham testified, he was given a rough time. He was enraged, and said so: "My testimony has been twisted and turned by innuendo, by implication and by every unfair means . . . [so as to make it] appear that I entered some sort of corrupt bargain. . . . I resent it and I shall resent it to the end of time."

Bingham could not believe what was being done to him; he was horrified that some senators would "condescend to such a low level and use cheap insinuation to damage the reputation of a fellow Senator."

Privately, Bingham admitted that it had been a mistake to bring Eyanson into the closed tariff meeting, and he regretted the fact that his "fairly thin skin" made him speak out so furiously against other senators. He could probably have escaped with only mild embarrassment if he had openly admitted his error, apologized for it, and then kept his mouth shut. Even his harshest critics acknowledged that what he had done was really more of a technical violation of the rules than anything else. But Bingham's honor had been insulted and he could not bear that. He was incapable of humbling himself. It was much the same sort of reaction he had when in 1915

Peruvian officials had accused him of stealing gold from Machu Picchu. He could not bear that there were those who tried "to make the outside world believe I was guilty of moral turpitude."

Though he knew he was wrong, in public Bingham could admit to no stain on his honor and could only lash out against his critics. On November 4, 1929, Republican Senator George W. Norris moved that his fellow Republican be censured: "RESOLVED that the action of the Senator from Connecticut . . . is contrary to good morals and senatorial ethics and tends to bring the Senate into dishonor and disrepute and such conduct is hereby condemned." It was a strong resolution.

After a debate the resolution was adopted by a vote of 54 to 22. The adoption of this resolution by so overwhelming a margin was a stunning slap in the face to the proud Bingham. There had not been a resolution of censure passed in the Senate for nearly 30 years. The last one was to censure a couple of hot-tempered senators who had actually gotten into a fistfight in the Senate chamber.

What was most painful about the vote, as far as Bingham was concerned, was the lopsided majority by which it had passed. That 32 Democrats in the Senate would have voted for it could be explained away. They were the opposition and ready to seize on any pretext to embarrass the party in power. But 22 Republicans had also voted to censure; as many Republicans had voted for censure as had voted against it.

It is true that some of the Republicans like Norris were Progressive Republicans who felt betrayed by Bingham. The patron saint of the Progressive Republican movement was former President Theodore Roosevelt. While Bingham had started as a great admirer of TR, he had moved steadily rightward. Yet even those who agreed with Bingham politically had not spoken out strongly in his defense. The truth was that Hiram Bingham had inherited his grandfather's talent for irritating people—and his colleagues in the Senate didn't like him very much. Many were just waiting for the opportunity to bring him down. With the Eyanson affair, Bingham had handed them their chance on a silver platter, and they took it. The newspapers described Bingham, arriving for the Senate vote as "white faced but smiling." He left the Senate chamber after the vote still white faced, but unsmiling. Later when asked about the censure he said, "Senators I understand not at all. I understand so much better the ethics and morals of explorers."

What was it about Hiram Bingham III that made him so widely disliked in the Senate? His grandfather had generated a great deal of hostility by projecting an air of moral superiority to those around him. Senator Bingham felt himself to be intellectually and socially superior to the other senators, and he never bothered to hide his feelings. Always the professor, he would not hesitate to correct a colleague when he made an error in Latin or Spanish. He was openly critical of those senators who had to "play to the galleries, to undertake things that will bring them into the headlines." He conveniently overlooked the fact that as the man who landed on the White House lawn in an autogyro he was one of the most skillful and successful grandstand players and headline hunters in the Senate.

He was not comfortable with the idea of open primaries for senator, preferring that candidates be chosen, as he had been, from among "the most qualified members of society." In fact, Bingham wasn't really comfortable with the idea of elected senators at all, and he occasionally referred to himself as the "Ambassador from Connecticut."

Bingham's haughty attitude toward his Senate colleagues was wickedly but accurately satirized in an article entitled "A Superior Person" by Duff Gilfond, which appeared in the popular publication *American Mercury* in March of 1930, after the censure vote. With tongue firmly in cheek, Gilfond described Bingham as "a suave elegant gentleman whose entire career has been as perfect as his face," as one having a "clean-cut classical countenance crowned by a gorgeous head of silver," and as one who "can speak with few, hobnob with fewer." The article referred to Bingham as the "tallest, stateliest, most god-like" member of the Senate, and in a striking phrase, stated that "[o]ne of the most impressive scenes in the Senate is the procession of His Lordship, his tiny wife and his seven stalwart sons filing out of the Senate gallery. . . ."

Gilfond also satirized the hypocrisy of other senators who had been guilty of the same sins as Bingham, and worse, yet who now rose up in mock moral indignation against him, because at some point in the past Bingham had snubbed them.

After his censure, Bingham resolved that he would never resign from the Senate; but to ease the pain of the insult, he did what he usually did in such situations—he took a long trip. This time he went to Samoa and was away from the Senate for months.

Not only did Bingham not resign, he resolved to stand for reelection in 1932. He based his campaign on a new issue, not aviation or U.S. overseas territories but Prohibition. Prohibition—the forbidding of the manufacture, transportation, and sale of most alcoholic drinks—had become the law of the land, and Bingham was against it. The Prohibition Amendment had been ratified in 1919, and in fairness it should be stated that Bingham had never liked it. It was one of the few points of major disagreement between Bingham and President Calvin Coolidge. In general, the Republicans were the "drys," who favored Prohibition, while Democrats were the "wets," who tended to oppose it. But on this subject, Bingham had always been out of step with his party. By 1932 Bingham not only favored the repeal of Prohibition but also became a national leader of the anti-Prohibition movement. He wrote and spoke extensively on the subject. "When it comes to what they wear, what they eat and what they drink people generally like to do as their ancestors have done," he said. He called for outright repeal of the Eighteenth, or Prohibition, Amendment at the 1932 Republican National Convention. According to the *New York Times*, Bingham appealed to "the dripping wet vote."

This was certainly not what Bingham's ancestors would have done. If such a thing were possible, Hiram senior, who was able to have liquor banned in Hawaii, and Hiram junior, who was constantly admonishing his son about the drinking habits he had picked up at school, would be spinning in their graves at the sight of a Bingham leading the fight for "demon rum."

By 1932 the nation had turned against Prohibition, but that turn wasn't strong enough to save Senator Bingham's seat. He lost to Democrat Augustine Lonergan by 7,745 votes. In the 1932 election the Democrats led by Franklin D. Roosevelt swept the Republicans led by Herbert Hoover out of office in a landslide. Bingham's close loss indicates that he still retained a considerable reservoir of goodwill in Connecticut.

Yet six years earlier he had won by nearly 80,000

votes. What caused this turnaround? Partly, perhaps mainly, it was the times. The stock market had crashed in 1929, and by 1932 the country was in the grip of the Great Depression. The sort of conservative economic politics supported by President Hoover and Senator Bingham had fallen out of favor. Bingham's rather aristocratic notions about who should lead the country ran counter to FDR's popular doctrines about the value and wisdom of the "common man." The censure vote in the Senate didn't help either. The 1932 election essentially ended Hiram Bingham's once promising political career.

After his election defeat, Bingham continued to linger about Washington, D.C., taking a number of high-paying business positions of the type that are usually available to well-connected former senators. He also kept up his academic connections by writing a massive biography of Elihu Yale, the benefactor of his old alma mater. He would get up to denounce President Franklin Roosevelt and the New Deal to small audiences of like-minded conservatives. When World War II broke out, he was called upon to lecture to sailors about to be sent to the South Sea Islands, for that was a part of the world that he knew well. That was his main contribution to the war effort in World War II. Bingham was no longer the man to "keep an eye on" that he had been when he first entered the U.S. Senate.

Up to now very little has been said of Alfreda Bingham and the seven Bingham sons. The reason is that from shortly after his marriage Hiram Bingham spent most of his time away from his family, either on his foreign travels or busy with his military and political careers.

Alfreda Bingham was a small, plain-looking woman

who stood, quite literally, in the shadow of her tall, elegant, and famous husband. Despite the fact that she was the real source of the Bingham fortune, she was very much a woman of her times. She regarded herself primarily as a companion and inspiration for her husband rather than as an independent person. For his part, Bingham showered his wife with affectionate, even adoring, letters sent from South America, France, Samoa, or wherever he happened to be at the time. He told her that her personal contact with their sons was "so much better for them than mine" because she was a more compassionate person. He repeated that he had "placed her on a pedestal" and that he "worshipped" her. Bingham also commented, "Our married life has really been far happier than most because there have been many long periods of separation."

But family life was not as placid as Bingham wished to make it seem. When he was away from the family, Hiram Bingham rarely lacked for female companionship. Indeed, as early as 1927 he put the matter quite bluntly to his shocked wife: "I think it would be wise if you encouraged me to see more of other women and liked me to have as good a time with them as I thought best." Alfreda did not quite see it that way, and over the next decade the strains in the Bingham family became increasingly severe. Alfreda found her position "on a pedestal" very uncomfortable.

Hiram and Alfreda were divorced in 1937, five years after Bingham's electoral defeat. Shortly after his divorce, Bingham married Suzanne Carol Hill, the former wife of one of his congressional colleagues and a woman with whom he had been having an affair since 1925.

Bingham's sexual attitudes and activities were not unusual for men of his class and time, but his puritanical missionary father and grandfather would have been horrified.

To the seven Bingham sons their father was always a remote figure. They lived primarily at the family mansion of Prospect Hill in New Haven, Connecticut. During the colder months they might be found at the family estates in Florida or Jamaica. They grew up in what one of them later called "a garden world"—very different from the near poverty of their father's boyhood in Honolulu.

All the Bingham boys were given educations typical of those of the scions of upper-class American families. Of the seven boys only one, Alfred Mitchell, strove to gain any public recognition. Like his father, Alfred went into politics. But while Hiram Bingham had moved increasingly to the political right, Alfred Bingham veered sharply leftward.

Alfred traveled around the United States trying to see how "the other half" lived, and it shocked him. While working at a factory in Connecticut, Alfred took a different name so that he would not be identified as the senator's son. In 1932 he took a world tour and visited the Soviet Union, which in many ways he greatly admired, though he never became a Communist.

Back in America he started a radical magazine called *Common Sense*. While Hiram Bingham criticized FDR from the right, Alfred Bingham criticized him from the left. Hiram Bingham looked at the first issue of *Common Sense*, tossed it across the room, and never looked at another copy. The magazine was largely supported by Bingham family money, though most of the other Binghams had no sympathy at all with Alfred's political views. What had happened was that the gap between

Hiram and the rest of his family had grown so wide that the Binghams tended to support Alfred just because he had so openly opposed his father. Alfred had really moved into the position of being head of the family, and other family members turned to him, rather than to the absent Hiram, for advice and guidance.

Alfred delivered what may have been the harshest and most cutting judgment of all upon his father when he wrote in his journal, "I am tolerant of mother but not of father because I feel mother's faults are ingrained by long training whereas father's seems to be a product of the demoralization of politics: and I had hoped he would be a great man."

Ultimately, there was a moderate emotional, though not political, reconciliation between father and son. Hiram came to look upon Alfred's concern for the poor and oppressed as the modern version of the missionary zeal that had driven the first two Hiram Binghams to try and convert the "heathens."

Hiram Bingham made one more brief appearance on the political scene. During the 1950s the United States was gripped by an anti-Communist hysteria that came to be known as McCarthyism, after one of its instigators, Senator Joseph McCarthy. People were hounded from their jobs not because of what they did but because of what they believed, and often merely because of what someone else said they believed. It was a disgraceful era in American history, and unfortunately Hiram Bingham played his part in it. In 1951 he was appointed chairman of the Loyalty Review Board of the Civil Service Commission. He declared that government employees should be dismissed not only on evidence of current disloyalty but also on the basis of what their past beliefs may have been.

There was a great irony in Bingham's position, for he would doubtless have had to dismiss his own son Alfred for espousing radical causes. And later his grandson Stephen would become not merely a radical, but a revolutionary who was accused of smuggling a gun to a radical prisoner who shot á guard. Stephen Bingham has been on the run from the FBI since 1971. Hiram Bingham did not live to experience the full impact of this irony, for he died on June 6, 1956.

The last thirty years or so of Hiram Bingham III's life were a disappointment, and in some ways a disgrace. When he abandoned his dream of finding cities of gold and took up a pursuit of political power, he may indeed have suffered a "demoralization," as his son Alfred believed.

But it isn't necessary to leave the story of Hiram Bingham on so depressing a note. For there was always Machu Picchu, and on that subject there is more to tell.

CHAPTER 11

Return to Machu Picchu

Hiram Bingham's career reached its high point figuratively, and almost literally, that July afternoon in 1911 when the young explorer first looked upon the "unbelievable dream" of the lost city of Machu Picchu. After that, and though it was not apparent at first, his career ran slowly but steadily downward. The more deeply enmeshed he became in politics, the more this downward slide picked up speed. Bingham had the qualities that made him a superb adventurer-explorer. He looked the part, and it was his part. But he only looked the part of senator; in that role he was grossly miscast.

At moments Bingham seemed to realize his unfitness for the political life: he himself remarked that he understood the morals of explorers but not the morals of senators.

In his book on the Bingham family, *Fathers and Sons*, historian Char Miller observed: "His [Bingham's] roles of aviator and public servant not only maintained the values of the explorer but never superseded Bingham's allegiance to that earlier career. His descriptions in *Who's Who in America* illustrate the point. In every edition between 1910 and 1932 he identified himself solely as an explorer. Between 1933 and the year of his death in 1956 he appended 'ex-Senator.' He could be out of politics, for it was merely an occupation, but he could never be a former explorer."

Though Bingham apparently always thought of himself first and foremost as an explorer, during his political years the numerous articles that were written about him barely mentioned Machu Picchu or his other discoveries. During the empty years that followed his political defeat, Bingham turned more and more to thinking and writing about the Inca world that he had found. In 1948 he revised and refined some of his previous writings on his explorations in a book called *Lost City of the Incas*. In this book Bingham finally presented his fully developed theory about the origins of Machu Picchu. The book is still widely read today, and though most authorities would disagree with Bingham's theories, few dispute the statement that it is one of the finest journals of exploration ever produced.

Perhaps Bingham's later life would have been different had it not been for the insult that he had received from the Peruvian government in 1915, when he was accused of stealing gold from Machu Picchu. Perhaps Bingham, who acknowledged having a "fairly thin skin," should not have reacted so violently and should have stuck with Peruvian exploration despite the rebuff.

It took the Peruvian government many years to realize what Bingham had found for them. Not only was Machu Picchu of enormous historical value, it had the potential of being an enormous tourist attraction as well—a romantic, intact ancient Inca city, in a most spectacular location. What more could people ask for?

Of course, even hardy tourists could not be expected to scramble up to Machu Picchu the way Bingham had, and a mule trail would find relatively few takers. So the government built a rail line down the Urubamba Valley to the foot of the mountains. There tourists transfer to a bus that snakes up what traveler and writer L. Sprague de Camp called "a terrifying switchback road to a tourist hotel perched amid the crags. Thence it is but a short walk to the ruins."

Despite the terrifying bus ride, and the fact that many tourists suffer grievously from the altitude, Machu Picchu is one of the premiere tourist attractions in South America. Each year thousands experience at least something of the thrill that Bingham felt when he first entered the "lost city."

The road to Machu Picchu was opened in 1948, and the Peruvian government invited Bingham to the opening ceremonies as guest of honor. The road was named, appropriately enough, Carretera Hiram Bingham. Though he once swore that he would never return to Peru, thirty years had dulled his anger, and Bingham attended the ceremonies and enjoyed them, as well as the honors that were showered upon him. He deserved the honors.

No matter what else happened in his life, no one could take away from Hiram Bingham that supreme moment of adventure and discovery, a moment that most people can only dream of, but that he had lived.

Bibliography

Bingham, Hiram, Sr. *A Residence of Twenty One Years in The Sandwich Islands.* Hartford, Conn.: Hezekiah Huntington, 1849.

Bingham, Hiram, III. *Across South America.* Boston: Houghton Mifflin, 1911.

————. *The Discovery of Machu Picchu.* New York: Harper, 1913.

————. *Elihu Yale: The American Nabob of Queen Square.* 2nd ed. Archon Books, 1968.

————. *An Explorer in the Air Service.* New Haven: Yale University Press, 1920.

————. *Inca Land: Explorations in the Highlands of Peru.* Boston: Houghton Mifflin, 1922.

————. *Journal of an Exploration Across Venezuela and Colombia, 1906–7.* New Haven: Yale Publication Association, 1909.

————. *Lost City of the Incas: The Story of Machu Picchu.* New York: Duell, Sloan and Pearce, 1948.

De Camp, L. Sprague, and De Camp, Catherine C. *Ancient Ruins and Archaeology.* Garden City, N.Y.: Doubleday, 1964.

Deuel, Leo. *Conquistadors Without Swords*. New York: St. Martin's, 1967.

Hemming, John. *The Conquest of the Incas*. New York: Harcourt Brace Jovanovich, 1970.

Miller, Char. *Fathers and Sons: The Bingham Family and the American Mission*. Philadelphia: Temple University Press, 1982.

Index